THE DIFFERENCE ENGINE

To our children, Eva, Tanya, Elena, Alexander and Samuel. May they grow up in a world of collaboration and tolerance.

The Difference Engine

Achieving Powerful and Sustainable Partnering

Anne Deering and Anne Murphy

G o w e r

Published by
Gower Publishing Limited
Gower House
Croft Road
Aldershot
Hampshire GU11 3HR
England

Gower
Old Post Road
Brookfield
Vermont 05036
USA

British Library Cataloguing in Publication Data
Deering, Anne
    The difference engine: achieving powerful and sustainable partnering
    1. Partnership 2. Organizational sociology 3. Strategic alliances (Business)
    4. Personnel management
    I. Title II. Murphy, Anne
    658'.042

ISBN 0566 08048 6

Library of Congress Cataloging-in-Publication Data
Deering, Anne, 1959–
    The difference engine: achieving powerful and sustainable partnering/Anne Deering and Anne Murphy.
        p. cm.
    Includes index.
    ISBN 0–566–08048–6 (hardcover)
    1. Communication in organizations.   2. Strategic alliances (Business)
3. Cooperativeness.   I. Murphy, Anne, 1955–.
II. Title.
HD30.3.D438   1998
658'.044–dc21   98–9612
                                                                           CIP

Typeset in 11/13 Palatino by Saxon Graphics Ltd and printed and bound in Great Britain by Biddles Ltd, Guildford and King's Lynn

The first 'Difference Engine' was the prototype of the modern computer, built by Charles Babbage in the 1820s. His machine was an assembly of cogs and wheels that solved equations by calculating the differences between sets of numbers. The Difference Engine we shall be describing in this book is the value-adding potential of partnerships that is latent in the differences between people and their organizations.

Contents

List of figures

Acknowledgements

Writing this book has been an act of creative partnership. Our debt of gratitude extends over a wide community of writers and thinkers too numerous to mention who have taken the trouble to set down their thoughts and share them, and who have helped to shape our thinking over the years.

For their unstinting generosity in sharing their research and for inspiring us with their energy in the search for new ways of seeing, we thank Chris Blantern, Tom Boydell, Bill Isaacs, Sandra Janoff, Michael Jones, Bob Lewis, Rose Trevelyan and Marvin Weisbord.

Our thanks also to the many members of the original research consortium, for sharing with us their partnering experiences and insights.

For their openness and the spirit of learning with which they shared their corporate stories, we thank Malcolm Johnson of SEEBOARD, Jose Mari Larrañaga of Mondragón Corporación Cooperativa, and Robin Saxby of ARM.

For their trust, in the early days of the research, and for sticking with us as we took the first steps towards the philosophy presented in this book, we thank Mike Ash-Edwards, Simon Carter,

Peter Cromer, John Higgins, Paul Joachim, Myriam Kamhi, David Keltie, Sally Randall, Graham Stevenson and Karen Winder. (There are others we would like to thank whom we cannot name without jeopardizing the anonymity of some of the case material.)

Most especially, our thanks go to Tom Lloyd for his extraordinary patience and expertise.

To our husbands, Angus and Fernando, for their support and encouragement in the precarious balancing act of combining work and home, our love and gratitude.

Introduction

Until a few years ago, the large, integrated organization was the undisputed king of the business jungle. Now, its crown is being contested by more sociable corporate creatures, hunting in packs. The intensity of competition is not abating – quite the contrary – but the primary competitive agent is changing. Co-operation is ceasing to be the opposite of competition, and is becoming instead one of its preferred methods.

It is no longer controversial to expound the idea that in many industries the main competitive agents in the future will not be the integrated organizations, but networks of independent players with complementary skills and resources linked together by shared objectives. Even people who remain convinced that, in their industries at least, the best way to assemble a particular set of resources is to buy those they lack cannot deny that elsewhere – in air travel, car-making and telecommunications, for instance – co-operation in the form of joint ventures, partnerships and so-called 'strategic alliances' has become an important, if not the dominant, strategic theme. According to some estimates, the rate at which American firms are forming partnerships has increased tenfold since 1970, and is still accelerating.

Many of those who profess a preference for buying rather than wooing partners are showing no reluctance to 'outsource' non-core functions, like computer systems management, accounting or distribution, to subcontractors or 'tactical' partners, and there is a growing realization that the only way to extract value from acquisitions is to treat them as partners, rather than possessions.

However, for an idea that has come to play such a significant role in mainstream strategic thinking in so many industries, and the merits of which are so widely acknowledged, the secrets of successful inter-organization co-operation – which we shall call 'partnering' – remain remarkably elusive.

Partnering is fine in theory, but too many alliances that have been billed as bold, resource-leveraging initiatives have foundered as a result of conflicts of interest and personalities or have absorbed huge amounts of management time for very little return for the practical case for partnering to have become universally indisputable.

Because partnerships end for reasons other than failure, it is difficult to assess the current partnership failure rate, but a reasonable guess is that barely one in three succeed in the sense that they fulfil their objectives and earn a return in excess of their cost of capital.

It is for this reason that acquisition, despite its attendant financial and cultural risks, is still seen by many business managers as the 'safest' way to secure and maintain access to the additional resources, competencies and markets that their increasingly global strategies demand. After a lull in merger and acquisition activity in the early 1990s, there has been a sharp mid-decade acceleration, as firms in industries facing turbulent futures, such as telecommunications, pharmaceuticals and banking, have acquisitively jockeyed for position.

Partnering is here to stay, however, and firms that adopt the acquisition strategy today may find themselves at a serious disadvantage tomorrow, compared to those who persevered with the partnership strategy and learned to tap the full power of the Difference Engine.

We believe that partnering relationships, both within and between organizations, will become the essence of the successful

21st-century corporation, and that what we are learning today in the partnership microcosm will be the key to success in tomorrow's business macrocosm. But the partnering model of business presents some formidable challenges to many conventional assumptions about strategy, communication and leadership, and will require new approaches, new tools and a new philosophy to help guide the 21st-century organization to self-transformation through partnering.

Participative research

The origins of this book date back to discussions within A.T. Kearney about the ways in which the traditional 'multi-unit business enterprise', as business historian Alfred Chandler called it, was being progressively eroded by the compulsion modern organizations evidently feel to operate beyond their boundaries.

What struck us about the well-documented partnering explosion was that it seemed to be taking place within a methodological vacuum. Many of our clients were zealous converts to the new creed of inter-firm collaboration, but it was clear to us that the hunger for partnerships, alliances and joint ventures was not matched by partnering skills, and that this was leading to serious indigestion as managers struggled with the cultural and relationship aspects of working across boundaries.

So we contacted a number of organizations who were interested in the topic, and proposed a joint research programme. The idea was that our partners would set the agenda to suit their own concerns and interests, and we would manage the programme in the hope that an exploration of their particular concerns would yield some general insights which should help us serve our clients.

The organizations identified a number of problems and issues of concern. They found it hard to understand their partners and to equip their people for both equal and unequal partnering relationships. They were worried about communications and the lack of opportunities to discuss strategic matters with their partners, and wanted a set of indicators to assess the health or otherwise of their partnering relationships. They wanted to know how to reconcile the human and operational aspects of partnering (for example, how to manage trust, ensure openness and create a collaborative atmosphere), and they were hungry for guidance on how to develop action-oriented relationships, robust enough to adapt to constantly changing circumstances.

We distilled these concerns into four research objectives:

- to develop improved inter-partner communications systems
- to find a usable partnering 'language'
- to identify the crucial dimensions of partnership
- to incorporate the language and dimensions in a methodology for analysing partnerships.

Following extensive qualitative and quantitative research, a set of common themes and issues emerged, and the Partnering Grid on which much of this book is based was born.

The participants worked collaboratively with the grid and the results of the research, and generated new questions that had to be addressed to test the validity of the concepts we were developing. The process of refinement continues, formally and informally, whenever anyone expresses an interest in using the Partnering Grid in a real work setting.

Throughout the project we have used a participative research method which assumes that knowledge acquisition and 'sense-making' are collective endeavours that should involve participants in the research in ways that ensure knowledge is generated with and for them, rather than merely about them. This is different from the traditional research method, which separates meaning from the research 'subjects' and uses them as 'objects' to be moved in and out of the research design irrespective of their local contexts.

We took the view that by focusing only on findings that were generally applicable, the traditional method denied research subjects an opportunity to learn about their own dilemmas and problems, and that a participative approach was therefore more appropriate for a partnering research programme. Moreover, we felt that a participative approach was also more likely to generate useful new insights and ideas, in an area where the failure of conventional approaches to yield much in the way of useful results has led to growing scepticism about partnering.

The journey ahead

The question that inspired us to write this book was: 'Can we discover a way into the soft core of partnering, from which a platform and a set of diagnostic tools can be derived to help those who believe in partnering's power to develop partnering competence?'

Our answers are: 'Yes, we can,' and 'Yes, we believe we have.' In the pages that follow, we hope to persuade the reader that we are right on both counts.

In Part I, 'Understanding partners', we present and explore a new way of thinking and talking about partnerships.

We argue in Chapter 1, 'A new kind of enterprise', that the explosion in business partnering in recent years heralds the end of the era of 'integrated enterprise' and the beginning of the era of 'partnership enterprise'. We will suggest that 'globalization' and the convergence of technology oblige all organizations to seek partners among alien cultures.

We will identify the main drivers of the partnering trend, and review the prescriptive management literature on partnering.

Business people have been taught (hence most of them believe) that harmony is not only desirable but also vital in business relationships. They have no training in managing partnerships between radically different cultures, and have not learned to explore the differences between them and their partners without feeling compelled to try to eradicate them.

In Chapter 2, 'A new language for partnering', we present a solution we have devised to the problem of talking about and analysing inherently non-harmonious relationships. We call it the Partnering Grid (see page 26). It was developed during our partnering research project, and takes the form of a two-by-three matrix of perceptions, defined by *ambition* on the y-axis, and *perceptions of difference* on the x-axis.

We, and many of those who have used the grid, believe that it provides a language for discussing partnering and partnership perceptions that is simple and illuminating. (Some say it is the most powerful tool they have so far come across for this purpose.)

Chapter 3, 'The origins of the grid', is rather technical, and can be skipped without affecting the reader's ability to follow the main argument. It describes how a number of ideas and theories about organizational learning and activity, individual psychology and complex systems have contributed to the development of the grid, and been embedded in it. We will suggest that although contemporary management thinking has benefited greatly from such interdisciplinary adventures, it remains locked in a 'modernist' paradigm that is incapable of accommodating the ambiguities and paradoxes characteristic of the modern world.

We will argue that the objective of much modern theory on the so-called 'learning organization' has been to learn enough about human behaviour to be able to manipulate it. In other words, learning is usually seen as a way to eliminate rather than transcend difference. Our view is that in the real world there is too much that divides partners who are brought together by globalization and technological convergence, and that the real task of learning is to enable organizations to form alliances and other relationships where neither control nor harmony is achievable.

In Chapter 4, 'Searching for "fit"', we explain how the grid can remove the blockages that afflict partnerships struggling with apparently irreconcilable differences, and show how it locates partnership perceptions, and how individuals who have located themselves on the grid can deduce where other parties to the relationship are 'coming from'.

In Part II, 'Acting on common ground', we focus on the right-hand side of the grid, where partnerships in which both power and knowledge are widely distributed are obliged to move, and we explore the implications for management.

In Chapter 5, 'Living with difference', we suggest that in many modern partnerships, valuing difference is clearly a more practical approach than searching in vain for harmony. We call the approach 'searching for common ground', and argue that although it requires the adoption of a new attitude to management, it is worth mastering because it opens up a much wider 'opportunity set' for prospective partners.

Chapter 6, 'Exploring common ground', discusses what seems to us to be a major implication of the new era of partnering: that enterprise strategy cannot be centrally planned or 'intended' in the traditional way, but must be allowed to 'emerge' from the exploration of common ground. We will argue that partnership strategy, if it deserves the name, takes the form of a series of projects, and that this granular nature of emergent strategy makes partnerships more adaptable and more creative than conventional integrated enterprises.

In Chapter 7, 'Trading in "common" sense', we suggest that conventional business communications are both inefficient and ineffective, because they are based on monologue. We advocate the adoption of the 'philosophy of dialogue'. We suggest such an approach will exploit far more of the networking potential offered by modern information technology (IT), and we explain how the process of developing a dialogue-based IT system will reveal much of what the old, 'monologue' communications model obscures.

In Chapter 8, 'Somebody at the helm', we suggest that the nature of leadership changes dramatically in situations where power is very widely distributed. We refer to new research on leadership in academic scientific research groups as a model in microcosm for the knowledge-based partnering organizations of the future. Extrapolating from this research, we suggest that the main role of the leader, or leadership system, in a partnership context is to act as a 'container', within which the creativity inspired by the Difference Engine can flourish.

Chapter 9, 'On trust and conflict', considers the roles of trust and conflict in our model of partnering, and we end the book with some general principles that summarize our argument and prescriptions.

In the interests of maintaining the fluidity of the narrative, we have included case studies at the ends of some chapters: 'Stories from the front'. We make no attempt to direct the reader to important points, however, because we have no way of knowing what the 'important points' are for individuals. Make of the cases what you will – we have found all of them illuminating in one way or another.

The Partnering Grid plays an important role in the book, and we are anxious that it should be used as well as understood. To this end we have included an exercise in Appendix A that allows readers to apply the grid to their own situations.

Anyone interested enough in the subject of partnering to take the time to read this book is already engaged in a joint research programme with us. We therefore invite readers who complete the exercises and come up with results they find surprising, useful or illuminating to share them with us (with the names deleted or disguised, if necessary). In return, we undertake to send them periodic bulletins summarizing what we have learned. Anne Deering can be contacted at A.T. Kearney Ltd, Landsdowne House, Berkeley Square, London W1X 5DH; Anne Murphy can be contacted at anne@oyon.demon.co.uk via e-mail.

One of the axioms of partnering lore – to which this book is a contribution – is:

When we learn together, we learn more, we learn more quickly
and we can have more confidence in what we learn.

Part I
Understanding partners

1 A new kind of enterprise

An ability to create value through the skilful management of portfolios of partnering relationships is increasingly seen as a major source of competitive advantage. Some believe that it will be an essential business competence by the end of the millennium.

This trend reflects not an inexplicable outbreak of corporate gregariousness, but a belief that in today's rapidly changing and ever more complex environment, companies must look beyond their corporate boundaries and seek joint potential.

The idea that a constantly accelerating rate of change in the business environment is all we can be certain of these days is now so widely accepted it has become a cliché. Some say the new era of explosive, unpredictable change has been triggered by the growing intensity of global competition; others see it as the inevitable consequence of technological convergence. Some are anxious about it; others see it as a source of opportunity as old barriers are pulled down.

However it is explained and perceived, the daily reality for practically everyone in this era of rapid change is working with a bewildering, rapidly proliferating array of different possibilities, cultures, visions, agendas, opportunities and threats. And there's no agreement about what to do. While we are being bombarded by the fact of change, we are being deafened by a cacophony of different and frequently conflicting views about what it means, and what its management implications are.

This does not just apply to business. The world is locked in conflict and contradiction. Even mature democracies are struggling to cope with the problems change generates, such as youth violence, social fragmentation and ethnic isolation. Faith in the old dream of social integration and harmony is fading. We may wish it were not so, but we have no option but to learn to live with it.

Despite the constant, heroic attempts to reach across the old divisions and forge new partnerships to address unemployment and other pressing social and economic problems, the division persists, and the bridge-builders and mediators are regarded, for the most part, with cynicism and apathy. People seem, if not content with their difference and disagreements, at least under no great pressure to resolve or settle them.

While company leaders still dream of integration and harmony, changing markets, growing customer choice, the communications explosion and, above all, changing patterns of 'stakeholder' influence are painting a picture that is far too complex for the single monoculture organization to cope with on its own.

Organizations of all kinds are having to face up to the fact that the old monolithic bureaucracies are being progressively disempowered by the multitude of different, often conflicting voices, creeds, philosophies and agendas of modern social and economic discourse. The 'control' that bureaucracies were designed to exercise is slipping from their grasp, because the systems in their charge are becoming too complex and unpredictable.

Reading between the lines of the contemporary business debate reveals two theories about how organizations might respond to the loss of control.

The first is that the problem lies not with bureaucracies and control systems themselves, but with their relative lack of sophistication. According to this view, the growing complexity of the environment has outstripped the competence of control systems, but this is a technical problem, and control can be reasserted with the help of modern information technology and some minor system modifications. This theory assumes that control is desirable, and that the problem is how to achieve it.

The other, newer theory employs so-called 'double-loop learning' (Argyris and Schon, 1978), and questions whether 'control', in the old sense – even if it were achievable, which is doubtful – any longer serves a useful purpose. This is such a disturbing idea that it is rarely articulated in business and management debates, but it is hard not to see a tacit acceptance of it in the recent rapid growth in the rate at which companies are forming partnerships. For, in adopting partnering strategies, firms are acknowledging that, in practice if not yet in theory, the need for control is now less pressing than the need to form networks of relationships that are flexible enough to respond quickly to unpredictable and often conflicting demands.

The flight from control

In the *Wall Street Journal*, *The Financial Times* and *Reuters News – Far East*, mentions of partnerships, joint ventures and strategic alliances quadrupled between 1987 and 1995, despite a sharp slow-down in growth during 1990–92, when recession was focusing management's attention on internal matters (see Figure 1.1).

A recent study by Booz-Allen & Hamilton (1995) showed that the heightened interest reflected an explosion of joint ventures, licensing agreements, collaborative research, technology exchanges and marketing alliances over the past decade. Booz-Allen said that US companies formed only 750 such partnerships in the 1970s, but are now forming thousands each year. The study estimated that the top 1000 US companies now drew 6% of their revenues from alliances, compared to 1.5% in 1987, and concluded that the extraordinary growth in partnering amounted to 'a new chapter in the evolution of free enterprise'.

Whatever the historical significance one attaches to the late-20th-century growth in business partnering, it clearly poses new management challenges. Networks of autonomous systems are

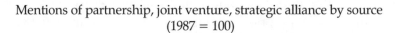

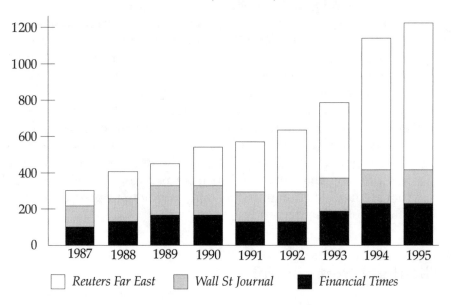

Figure 1.1   Partnering: a theme of our times

far more complex and less easily guided than integrated enterprises, and in an age when the shelf-life of knowledge is often
shorter than the time it takes an organization to capture, let alone
make sense of it, traditional guidance systems are worse than
useless. A wholly new style of management is needed to accommodate the lack of control in partnership enterprises, and their
complexity, as well as the speed with which decisions now have
to be taken.

Moreover, at the heart of this learning challenge is the need to
confront contradiction and paradox. For example, how can we
work with very different cultures, experiences and values, and
yet retain our sense of self? How can we marry a sense of corporate identity with the flexibility needed to work with very different ways of managing and doing business in local contexts? How
can we empower partners and other stakeholders (including our

own employees) to grasp opportunities without causing chaos? How can we foster trust and understanding, and retain a proper balance of power? How can we share without risking exploitation? How can we be open to influence, and yet sure of our identity? How can we achieve change when no one partner controls every aspect of the problem? And how can we share visions if we see things differently and see different things?

So far, most attempts to meet such challenges have focused on defence. Firms have partnered with or acquired other firms to strengthen their defences, and have accordingly concentrated on ensuring their partners and acquired firms are of the right size and shape to be bricks and buttresses in their battlements.

What they have failed to recognize is that each brick dreams of being a castle in its own right, and that the real essence of the new partnering architecture is not the bricks, but the mortar that both separates and unites them.

Joseph Badaracco (1993) and others have argued that to confine the new partnering model to purely defensive deployment is to deny its true potential and significance. Badaracco describes the autocratic management style of post-war US companies as a creature of the medieval 'Citadel Paradigm', which he says must be replaced by what he calls the 'City-State Paradigm' of Renaissance Italy: 'Against the broad sweep of the history of commerce and business organization, companies as citadels – clearly defined zones of ownership and control, surrounded by market relations – are the anomaly.'

The need for speed also favours the partnering enterprise. In a recent book, Catherine Alter and Jerald Hage (1993) say that 'multi-lateral arrangements, among diverse organizations that band together to produce a single product', are emerging as a major new form of enterprise, because they adapt more quickly and creatively to changing technologies and markets.

So modern business leaders have a clear choice: either try to apply traditional management principles of control to the new partnership enterprises, and risk disintegration; or find ways to collaborate without control, and risk chaos.

But, given the complexity of the modern business environment, the disappearance of traditional frontiers and the escalating battle for competitive advantage, this is really no choice at all, because going it alone is ceasing to be an option. For all sorts of reasons, to do with technology, competition, politics and access to resources, it is becoming imperative in a growing number of industries to seek new knowledge and capability through partnering. It is the only way to operate in increasingly competitive and liberal markets, and the only way to detect and respond sufficiently quickly to the wishes of increasingly diverse, demanding and capricious customers.

Partnering purposes

The inspirations of partnerships are legion, but the strategic drivers that frame and inform the decision to partner can be classified under four main headings:

Technology

The exploitation of technological advance has been a powerful impetus for partnering since long before James Watt linked his engineering genius to the entrepreneurial and managerial brilliance of Matthew Boulton in the 18th century, to develop and market his steam engine.

In recent times, partnerships between innovative small firms and large companies strong in marketing were being advocated as alternatives to licensing agreements at the height of the microelectronics revolution in the mid-1970s (Hlavacek et al., 1977), and a decade later such David and Goliath partnerships were being proclaimed as a good way for small, high-tech firms to establish themselves abroad (Berlew, 1984).

The way in which technological advance transcends traditional industry borders also provides a powerful partnering impetus. Yoshino and Rangan (1995) described how the inability of AT&T, Apple, Motorola, Sony, Matsushita and Philips to develop new 'personal intelligent communications' software led them to bury the competitive hatchet (Motorola and AT&T are rivals in wireless communications, and Philips, Sony and Matsushita compete in consumer electronics), and become co-investors in General Magic (see page 18).

Technological collaboration is also being increasingly widely used by groups of often competing companies, to establish and promote a technical standard, such as the VHS video standard, and Europe's GSM digital mobile phone system (see page 19).

Strategy

Although the exchange of skills and resources, and the desire for access to distant markets, remain important inspirations, the case for partnering has since become much wider. It has been promoted as a suitable response to large, periodic plate-shifts in the world economy (the disintegration of the Communist bloc, the integration of Europe, the opening up of China, etc.), the progressive globalization of markets and the convergence of consumer needs (Ohmae, 1989).

Partnering has also been advocated and used as an instrument of corporate restructuring. In one variation on this theme, the vendor firm sells a minority stake in a non-core business, and promises to sell the rest at some future date, so forming a temporary partnership with the buyer. This allows buyers to get to know prospective subsidiaries far more intimately than would otherwise be possible before paying the full price, and offers sellers the chance to earn a better price for the rest of their shares by ensuring a smooth, jointly managed transfer of control (Nanda and Williamson, 1995). The joint venture between Whirlpool and Philips, which led to the former's acquisition of the whole of the latter's 'white goods' business, was an example of a temporary partnership of this kind.

Value chain optimization

Another important theme of modern partnering is the idea that if traditional, market-based relationships between suppliers and purchasers were transformed into more intimate alliances, both parties could benefit. The idea was first promoted as a way of exerting control over the value chain that avoided the problems associated with the traditional strategy of vertical integration. It was cheaper and less risky, it was argued, to ally with suppliers than to buy them, and moreover, much could be learned from distributors about the needs of final customers (Narus and Anderson, 1986).

The argument was then generalized into a prescription to form value-adding partnerships (VAPs): groups of independent firms that collaborate to manage flows of goods and services along the whole value chain. Johnston and Lawrence (1988) described how McKesson, a US distributor of drugs, healthcare products and other consumer goods, was driven to develop a VAP by the business the major national drugstore chains were taking from the independent drugstores McKesson served.

Some saw the interest in value and supply chain management as a belated recognition of the merits of the Japanese *keiretsu* ('business society') system (Ferguson, 1990). Others argued that Western firms have already gone further than the *keiretsu* and developed a new form of enterprise, in which groups of firms – linked together in large umbrella networks through various kinds of alliances, ranging from formal equity joint ventures to loose, informal collaborations – coalesce and compete with each other (Alter and Hage, 1993; Gomes-Casseres, 1994).

Politics

As we have already seen, political institutions or government agencies sometimes play the role of sponsors or catalysts of corporate partnerships.

Japan's Ministry of International Trade & Industry (MITI) was an active sponsor of the successful attacks of Japanese firms on several major world markets over the past two decades, and the European Commission was a promoter of both the Prometheus and GSM projects (see pages 17 and 19).

Some have even argued that national and regional governments can and should sponsor partnerships between local companies, to 'organize' competition, and so avoid suicidal, head-to-head confrontations in increasingly liberal global markets (Urban and Vendemini, 1992).

The June 1996 agreement between Japanese and European microchip makers to 'organize' global trade in semiconductors was billed as a private sector initiative, but it was known that the European Commission and MITI approved of and helped arrange the meeting between representatives of NEC and Toshiba of Japan, Siemens of Germany and the Franco-Italian group SGS-Thomson that led to agreement of the pact.

But despite such occasional experiments in neo-protectionism, the general trend is towards more liberal trade. Governments have frowned on the anti-competitive partnering that occurred during the age of trusts, cartels and price-fixing. Although some embattled CEOs may still yearn for them, anti-trust laws and institutions have outlawed such 'agreements in restraint of trade'. No CEO will admit that attempts to fix prices or enter into anti-competitive agreements are acceptable or even effective responses to modern competitive pressures.

Most modern partnering is designed not to reduce competitive pressures, but to enhance the ability of partner companies to respond to them.

Conventional prescriptions

It is one thing to be convinced of the merits of a partnering strategy, and quite another to become adept at realizing the full potential of partnerships. For although the prospect of outstanding results from synergy and co-creation is often the inspiration for partnerships, the everyday experience is all too often of defensive behaviour and scepticism, leading to conflict and failure. Research by A.T. Kearney suggests that 50% of strategic alliances and as many as 80% of supply chain partnerships fail to add value.

It is not clear from either the literature or the graveyard of defunct partnerships why the mortality rate is so high. Explanations vary, the critics disagree, injured parties lick their wounds in private, and the sceptics see the failures as evidence that the whole idea of partnering is flawed. In the absence of a proven model for diagnosing partnering problems, we have to put them down to ill-defined personality conflicts – both individual and organizational.

There is no shortage of good advice as to what can and should be done to improve partnering relationships. Numerous books and articles have been published in recent years, with lists of principles that the authors claim will identify and remedy soft partnership ailments (Hamel, Doz and Prahalad, 1989; Moss Kanter 1994; Carlisle and Parker, 1989; Moody, 1994; Perlmutter and Heenan, 1986).

Four main prescriptions emerge from this literature:

1 **Ensure compatible values:** partners must focus on the long term, share benefits, deal fairly with each other, and try to find a common set of values.
2 **Adopt co-operative management styles:** collaboration should be embedded in joint improvement efforts, contacts between partner organizations at every level, and in agreed goals.
3 **Know each other's businesses:** partners should be open with each other and share strategies.
4 **Share information:** partners should ensure the free two-way flow of business information at all times.

This is sound advice, and resonates well with the perceptions and experiences of many involved in successful partnerships. But it is hard to disentangle cause and effect here: to decide whether partners who apply the four principles do so naturally because they happen to get on, or whether they get on because they have applied the principles.

Commentators usually assume it is the good principles that engender the good practice, but they cannot prove it, and it is sometimes hard to escape the suspicion that this conclusion is as much a consequence of the widespread though often tacit belief that every organizational problem has an organizational solution as it is the result of objective observation.

The prescriptions are essentially technical. All relationship issues are treated as problems, to which there are generally applicable solutions. There is so much of this kind of advice about how to foster good partnering, and it is being applied with such enthusiasm, that it is easy to forget that it all assumes the relationship is sound in the first place.

When trust itself is in doubt or absent, such prescriptions are inappropriate and ineffective. Their logic begins with an ideal of the harmonious relationship that is, in most cases, quite impossible to aspire to, let alone to achieve.

If all the conventional partnering nostrums can say when two or more different corporate cultures come together to pursue joint objectives is that conflict is bad and harmony should be sought, they offer very little that is of much practical use to most real partnerships.

There is a need for a more realistic kind of advice, helpful to those managing the vast majority of partnerships, where total harmony and complete trust are, and will remain, conspicuous only by their absence.

Partnership enterprise

We believe that most of the problems companies are experiencing in their partnerships are due to the fact that the new model of partnership enterprise is quite different from the old multi-unit enterprise, and requires a different set of principles to make it work.

Managers realize that the old, integrated structure, with its hierarchy and 'functional silos', must be replaced by flatter, process-based architectures, extending beyond their corporate boundaries. But these new architectures demand a loosening of conventional control systems within and between organizations, and this has brought 'soft' issues of trust, understanding and perception into sharp relief – issues which are much more complex and subtle than the issues managers of the 'old school' have ever had to deal with.

The problems firms encounter in partnering are special cases of general management problems, associated with relationships within, as well as between, organizations. Even organizations that have shunned the partnering strategy are struggling with the effects of downsizing on employer–employee 'contracts', the dilemmas created by their desire to empower people while continuing to control and direct them, and the need they feel to formulate inspiring visions and develop winning strategies at a time when today's assumptions are almost always belied by tomorrow's events.

There is a general acceptance of the need for new 'enterprise architectures' such as 'flat', 'horizontal' and process-based structures (as well as partnership enterprise), but there is, as yet, little understanding of the implications of these new architectures for management systems and styles.

We believe that the new enterprise architectures require not only a new style of management, but a new management philosophy. Much sensible and valuable advice has emerged from academics and management practitioners in recent years about the need for empowerment and the changing role of leadership, but most of it is based on what we regard as an outdated philosophy of management that misses the central point about organizations and enterprises – that they must operate effectively, despite the fact that in every walk of life, conflict and differences of opinion about how things are and what should be done are characteristic of the modern world.

The new enterprise architectures are not as 'controllable' as the old, and we believe that visions, missions and harmonization programmes will be no more effective at controlling them than the old command and control approach.

Even if 'harmony' was useful in business relationships, it is simply not attainable these days, and there is good reason to believe that attempts to achieve it can actually be harmful. The search for 'harmony' to reduce conflict and promote trust in business relationships is the wrong solution to the wrong problem, for when we insist on seeing all partnering problems in terms of trust and conflict, we have to accept that they can never be solved. There will always be issues of trust and conflict to deal with, so until managers learn to see relationships in different ways, they are doomed to squander their efforts on a hopeless quest.

Trust and conflict are important, and we will have more to say about them at the end of the book. That is where they belong. They are *epiphenomena*: they are consequences, not causes. In the thesis we shall develop in the intervening chapters, they do not play a major role. Trust and an absence of conflict are not pre-conditions for successful partnering, as they're usually alleged to be; they emerge from successful partnering.

Our task in this book is to present an alternative framework for perceiving, thinking about and working with relationships that will reveal new possibilities for action in this new age of 'partnership enterprise'.

In Chapter 2 we will describe our Partnering Grid, a two-by-three matrix that at first sight looks very like the sort of matrix beloved of the 'old' management, but which actually incorporates a radically new management philosophy.

Before we do that, however, we want to put partnering into a historical perspective, because what we are proposing here is not a new, but a forgotten form of enterprise: until the mid-19th century, partnership enterprise was the commonest form of enterprise.

Enterprise architecture on the American railroads

Pulitzer Prize-winner Alfred Chandler said (1977) that modern managerial capitalism began with a bang in October 1841, when two trains collided on the Western Railroad between Worcester and Albany. The conductor and a passenger died, and 17 others were injured.

The outcry that followed the accident led to an investigation of Western's operations by the Massachusetts legislature, and the appointment of a committee of inquiry which urged the line to assign 'definite responsibilities for each phase of the company's business, drawing solid lines of authority and communication for the railroad's administration, maintenance and operation'.

The implementation of this report led to what Chandler called 'the first modern, carefully defined, internal organizational structure used by an American business enterprise', and also 'the first American business enterprise to operate through a formal administrative structure, manned by full-time salaried managers'.

He called the system 'managerial capitalism', and identified a characteristic institution, 'the modern multi-unit business enterprise' (MBE), operated by a new kind of businessman, 'the salaried manager'.

But Chandler acknowledged that many railroads continued to be run in informal ways, without modern functional distinctions, internal auditing staff and sophisticated financial, capital and cost accounting systems, for many years. It was not until the 1880s that the procedural innovations became standard on all large American railroads.

One of the ironies of the early American railroads is that at the same time as they were giving birth to the MBE, they were experimenting with a very different form of organization that might have replaced the MBE before it became established.

The central weakness of the early rail systems was that railroads entering a terminal city had no direct links, and since they used different gauges and equipment, cars from one road could not be transferred onto another's track. In 1865 the Boston Board of Trade estimated that the cost of unloading and reloading freight between Boston and Chicago was over $500 000 a year.

The need to eliminate the high transhipment costs led to the standardization of gauges, equipment and procedures, and high levels of inter-firm co-operation. By the 1880s a rail shipment could move from one part of the country to another without a single transhipment.

The success of this inter-firm co-operation caused the American railroad network in the late 19th century to operate, for a while, as an interconnecting system resembling a modern value-adding partnership (see above).

Chandler said that such co-operation might have worked if managers had been more rigorous in maintaining agreed rates, and if cartel agreements had been legally enforceable. But the US Congress was in no mood to grant legal sanction to what most Americans saw as a form of price-rigging, and the 1887 Interstate Commerce Act forbade the pooling arrangements on which the brief period of co-operation depended. The scene was set for the battles between the speculators, led by Jay Gould (the 'Mephistopheles of Wall Street'), and the railroad system builders, led by the Vanderbilts.

We believe the wheel has now turned full circle, and that what we are witnessing today is the rediscovery of that model of inter-firm co-operation which flourished for a while on the US rail-roads in the mid-19th century. In other words, business is leaving the old era of 'managerial capitalism', in which the integrated multi-unit business enterprise was dominant, and is entering a new era of partnership enterprise.

Stories from the front

Prometheus

In 1987 the European Commission launched the eight-year, Ecu 900m Prometheus partnership between Europe's car, truck and electronic systems makers to develop new in-car systems that would reduce Europe's toll of 50000 road deaths a year.

Among numerous successful Prometheus projects were:

- a system with a dashboard video display and voice synthesizer that checks its accuracy via a geo-stationary satellite and shows and tells the driver where to go
- a windscreen sensing system that switches wipers on and off when it starts and stops raining
- ultra-violet head lamps, and head-up night vision displays
- a crash sensor that automatically reports a car's location to the emergency services
- intelligent cruise control that decelerates in response to messages from radar and infra-red systems about slow-moving traffic
- a video-imaging system that nudges drivers back on course when they stray across lane markings
- a video eye and head movement sensing system that detects driver fatigue.

The Prometheus programme was concluded in 1995, and erstwhile partners became competitors again in the rush to bring some of the fruits of their joint labours to market as quickly as possible, at prices motorists could afford.

General Magic

In January 1989, Apple Computer established a project to find business opportunities beyond traditional personal computing. The team decided to examine how people will need to deal with the complexities of everyday life in the 21st century. Code-named Paradigm and Pocket Crystal, the project evolved into a set of plans for products and services requiring expertise in computing, communications and consumer electronics. The team foresaw a new industry of personal intelligent communications (PIC).

It became clear that no one company could deliver all the PIC components, so in early 1990 Apple decided that the best way to pursue the vision was to set up an independent company. General Magic was incorporated on 1 May 1990. The founders, Marc Porat, Andy Hertzfeld and Bill Atkinson, attracted a team of people with experience in software and communications.

To ensure the new PIC technology became woven into the fabric of everyday life, General Magic sought to team up with firms well known for changing people's lives with new products and services.

In February 1991, Sony and Motorola joined Apple as investors in General Magic and licensees of its technology. AT&T joined the alliance in January 1992, Philips in November 1992, and Matsushita in January 1993. In 1994, Cable & Wireless, France Telecom, Fujitsu, Mitsubishi, Nortel, NTT, Oki, Sanyo and Toshiba also joined the General Magic Alliance.

General Magic's stated mission is to:

- Develop advanced enabling technologies, products and services that are powerful and immensely useful, yet always personal and pliable.
- License General Magic technologies to standard-setting hardware manufacturers and service providers that can bring the fruits of personal intelligent communications to the general public.
- Unleash the creativity of others by providing platforms that enable a broad range of developers and content providers to create new kinds of services, communicating applications, and hardware products.

Its stated vision is to create products and services that can help people to communicate, remember and know (source: General Magic's World Wide Web site, http://www.genmagic.com/index.html).

Setting standards

Few knowledgeable observers gave Groupe Spéciale Mobile (GSM) – a standard for digital mobile phone technology proposed by France Telecom and the German Bundespost in the early 1980s – much chance of being accepted by US companies, which favoured home-grown standards they could control more easily. However, the growth of GSM (developed collaboratively by European phone service operators and equipment makers at the urging of the European Commission) to become not merely the first pan-European standard for the business, but also a widely adopted standard in Asia and the Middle East, obliged the US industry to think again.

By avoiding the problems that had bedevilled standard-setting for the analogue mobile phone market, and creating a Continental standard to gain economies of scale for service operators and equipment manufacturers, GSM had achieved its two objectives by 1995, and had also helped to create a much larger market than would otherwise have been possible, so increasing competition and pushing prices down (*Financial Times*, 3 October 1995).

By that time, GSM had also become the dominant standard in many of the then fast-growing markets of Asia Pacific (but not in Japan, South Korea or Hong Kong), was well established in India and the countries of eastern Europe, and had gained access to the American market, in competition with Time Division Multiple Access (supported by AT&T) and Code Division Multiple Access (supported by Sprint). And because of the lack of a clear US standard and the predominance of GSM outside the USA, a number of small US telecommunications companies were throwing their weight behind GSM.

In time, of course, other technologies will supersede all the current standards, but Dataquest estimated that in 1999, GSM would still be by far the most widely accepted standard, in a world-wide digital cellular market which would be approaching 200 million subscribers (*Financial Times*, 3 October 1995).

Moreover, this successful European collaboration was expected to give the new Digital European Cordless Telephony system a very strong claim to be the second-generation global standard for digital mobile phones.

Summary

Business in the late 20th century is too complex and unpredictable to be managed by monolithic bureaucracies.

For this reason, business is entering a new era of what we call 'partnership enterprise'.

These looser enterprise architectures require a new management philosophy, to cope with the wider distributions of power and knowledge.

Organizations are adopting partnering strategies for a variety of reasons, but there is, as yet, no substantial body of partnering lore to guide them.

References

Alter, C. and Hage, J. (1993) *Organizations Working Together*, Sage.

Argyris, C. and Schon, D. (1978) *Organizational Learning: A Theory in Action Perspective*, Addison-Wesley.

Badaracco, J. (1993) *The Knowledge Link: How Firms Compete Through Strategic Alliances*, Harvard Business School Press.

Berlew, K. (1984) 'The joint venture: a way into foreign markets', *Harvard Business Review*, July/August.

Booz-Allen & Hamilton (1995) *A Practical Guide to Alliances*, Booz-Allen & Hamilton.

Carlisle, J. and Parker, R. (1989) *Beyond Negotiation: Redeeming Customer–supplier Relationships*, John Wiley.

Chandler, A. (1977) *The Visible Hand: The Managerial Revolution in American Business*, Harvard University Press.

Ferguson, C. (1990) 'Computers and the coming of the US keiret-su', *Harvard Business Review*, July/August.

Gomes-Casseres, B. (1994) 'Group versus group: how alliance networks compete', *Harvard Business Review*, July/August.

Hamel, G., Doz, Y. and Prahalad, C.K. (1989) 'Collaborate with your competitors, and win', *Harvard Business Review*, January/February.

Hlavacek, J., Dovey, B. et al. (1977) 'Tie small business technology to marketing power', *Harvard Business Review*, January/February.

Johnston, R. and Lawrence, P. (1988) 'Beyond vertical integration: the rise of the value-adding partnership', *Harvard Business Review*, July/August.

Moody, P. (1994) *Breakthrough Partnering: Creating a Collective Enterprise Advantage*, Oliver Wight.

Moss Kanter, R. (1994) 'Collaborative advantage: the art of alliances', *Harvard Business Review*, July/August.

Nanda, A. and Williamson, P. (1995) 'Use joint ventures to ease the pain of restructuring', *Harvard Business Review*, November/December.

Narus, J. and Anderson, J. (1986) 'Turn your industrial distributors into partners', *Harvard Business Review*, March/April.

Ohmae, K. (1989) 'The global logic of strategic alliances', *Harvard Business Review*, March/April.

Perlmutter, H. and Heenan, D. (1986) 'Cooperate to compete globally', *Harvard Business Review*, March/April.

Urban, S. and Vendemini, S. (1992) *European Strategic Alliances: Co-operative Strategies in the New Europe*, Blackwell.

Yoshino, M. and Rangan, S. (1995) *Strategic Alliances: An Entrepreneurial Approach to Globalization*, Harvard Business School Press.

2 A new language for partnering

We argued in Chapter 1 that the search for the harmony that nourished Chandler's multi-unit business enterprise in the one-and-a-half centuries it has dominated the business world has become a search for a chimera.

Harmonious relationships, where all parties – whether they are the employees or units of integrated enterprises, or members of the partnership enterprises that characterize the new era in the same way as the MBE characterized the old – are aligned and in concert with each other, are no longer available.

Almost all businesses are partnerships now, in spirit if not in fact, and given the complexity, volatility and diversity of partnering systems, seeking ideal relationships – even if such paragons exist, which we doubt – is not a practical partnering strategy.

We believe that in view of this intrinsic imperfectibility of partnerships, partners should devote less time and energy to harmonizing, aligning and reconciling, and more to trying to understand each other, and using such understanding to map out 'common ground'.

It was in this spirit of unbelief about the perfectibility of relationships that we undertook our research programme. We did not seek answers to such questions as 'What makes for a perfect partnership, how can it be achieved, and what steps and principles should guide partners in their search for it?', which one might have expected to be the aim of such research. Instead, we tried to understand how partners understand each other. We made no judgements about the merits or otherwise of the very different perceptions of partners within the same partnerships that emerged. We assumed that perceptions were real to their perceivers, and tried to discover how understanding and misunderstanding develop.

We therefore adopted a collaborative approach to the research, and because we did not know at the outset what would emerge, we tried to be as open-minded as possible. But you cannot just observe. A research programme cannot begin with no preconceptions or working hypotheses. Without even a rough idea of where you are going and what you may find, you have no basis for choosing where to look, for deciding what lines of inquiry to adopt, or for planning and orchestrating the research process.

The best research programmes are flexible and self-modifying, and often end up in surprising or unexpected places, but they all begin with conjectures and preconceptions, for without a few initial prejudices, they have nowhere to go.

We had to be confident that the research had the potential to generate useful 'thoughtware' for our practice: our partners in the research were hungry for insights into their problems, and we all wanted our findings to be sufficiently intriguing to arouse interest at a strategic level, but at the same time, to be practical and prescriptive enough to be applied in existing or emerging areas of business need.

Partnering is clearly a subject of great interest to managers of all kinds of organizations, and it is equally clear that it lacks a 'thought framework' to help diagnose and, if possible, remedy the causes of the frequent failures of partnerships.

We began with the belief that the fault lay not in partnering itself, but in the ways that partnerships are perceived and managed. We believed – and nothing we have learned during the research has shaken that belief – that partnering has enormous potential to create value.

It also seemed to us that the much looser control systems and structures involved in partnering, as opposed to ownership or merger, were sure to bring relationship issues such as trust into sharp relief. Process integration issues in partnerships have received quite a lot of attention already; we were much more interested in the human issue of working together across organizational rather than merely functional boundaries.

Much has been written about the importance of fostering trust relationships in de-layered, decentralized organizations, but most of it has focused on how to 'homogenize' cultures. Very little effort has been made to apply what we know about trust to relationships *between* rather than within organizations. Moreover, we felt – and still feel – that there is probably more to learn about trust from the study of relationships between organizations than from a study of relationships within them. For when there is no alternative to trust – when control is not an option – the need for trust is greater, and thus the search for it must be more diligent. When an organization's 'way of being' seems inappropriate, it can be changed, but the 'ways of being' of one's partners are, to all intents and purposes, inviolate. They cannot be changed; they can only be accommodated.

For this reason, we believe that much of what we have to say in this book has relevance for general management, not just for the management of inter-firm relationships. The modern emphasis on the processes rather than the structures of business makes it easy to see them as consisting as much, if not more, of relationships and partnerships between their members, component parts and units as of physical assets.

An organization has far more control over the partnerships it consists of, in this sense, than one independent partner has over another, but it is fast becoming an axiom of modern, 'soft' management that command and control are not as useful as they were – indeed, that they can be very dangerous tools, because to use and abuse them is to risk losing them.

There is also a cost consideration here. It is not enough to show that command and control is a 'practical' approach to management in an age where difference is all around us; it is also necessary to establish that it is 'affordable'. If there are other styles of management (and if there were not, there would be no point in writing this book), the need to 'police' command and control can make it appear an expensive solution to the problems of living and working together.

Trust has always been essential in co-operative relationships between organizations. These days, it is increasingly seen as essential in internal relationships, too. We have no 'recipe' for trust, however. It is the main glue that bonds modern, de-layered, decentralized organizations together, but it is the *consequence* of working well together, not its cause.

To be persuaded of the general relevance of these conclusions from our research, readers may like to apply the self-test in Appendix A to relationships *within* their organizations. It is based on the Partnering Grid that emerged from our research programme.

The Partnering Grid

The Partnering Grid plays a central role in this book. It is a new, and in our view (and the view of all those who have so far used it), an illuminating way of looking at relationships (including partnerships).

Anxious to cast our net as widely as possible, we collected a heterogeneous sample to study, including a major non-profit-making concern, divisions of two UK multinationals, a subsidiary of a state-owned French company, a large Swiss Bank, a privatized public utility, a self-styled 'virtual corporation' of consultants, an English metropolitan district council, a UK National Health Service trust and a civic retraining initiative.

Most people saw themselves as having been 'forced' into their partnerships by circumstances; they said that partnering was more to do with mutual benefit than a wish to co-operate and get on well. Conflict was seen as problematic but inevitable, and people had much to say about it, using words and phrases like 'adversarial', 'closing ranks', 'territory', 'empire-building', 'blame' (never theirs), 'distortion', 'inward-looking' and 'managing each other's expectations'.

They talked of 'power plays' and 'sitting on information'. They said it was crucial to keep control of the agenda through the customer, and many saw shared values as the best way to solve imbalances of power.

All our research partners said that problems of power and conflict were compounded by the fact that things were never as they appeared, or as their partners alleged, because there were always hidden agendas. In other words, most people felt their partnerships were too complex to be definable, and that it was impossible to get 'everything on the table'.

Five key insights emerged from the research:

1　Marginalization, not conflict, is what prevents partnerships from succeeding. The presence of conflict is not a sign of impending failure, and neither is its absence a guarantee of success.
2　Things are rarely what they seem. Expectations, perceptions and assumptions are the stuff of partnerships, and it is the complex interplay between them that determines whether a partnership succeeds or fails.
3　People associate partnering with 'harmony' and 'synergy'. Values such as trust, honesty and integrity are widely seen as vital, but harmony is often conspicuous by its absence. Most partnerships are characterized by some (often a great deal of) conflict, and threatening and defensive behaviour patterns are common.
4　Organizations manage this conflict in two basic ways: they try to offset the conflict by promoting positive values, or they try to reduce conflict directly by policing conformity or achieving sameness by seeking partners with very similar cultures.
5　Partners often see difference, rather than their response to it, as the underlying cause of conflict, but difference can also be a powerful source of creativity and transformation. In many cases it is the attempt to minimize difference and achieve 'alignment' that creates conflict, not difference itself.

These insights led us to develop what we call the Partnering Grid (see Figure 2.1). We will devote most of the rest of this chapter to describing it, and explaining the thinking behind it.

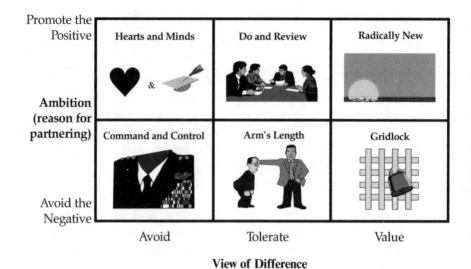

Figure 2.1   The Partnering Grid

Anatomy of the Partnering Grid

The grid is constructed by plotting the partner's view of and response to difference against the reasons for entering into the partnering relationship in the first place.

Every partnership is predicated on a partnership rationale or purpose, but the nature of these ambitions varies widely, from a wish to prevent negative outcomes (risk management) to the desire to promote positive outcomes (co-creation).

The labels on the six boxes in Figure 2.1 should not be seen as epitomes of their contents, but rather as short-hand mottoes, designed to facilitate discussion. Later in this chapter we will unpack the boxes a little, to give the labels more meaning.

Nor should it be assumed that there is an appropriate box for every partner organization. It is not possible – and neither, in our view, is it desirable – to confine a partner within one box, for different people in the same partner organization will always perceive the partnership in different ways. A box is not a place where a partnership is or wishes to get to; it is a place where an individual perceives it to be or wants it to move towards.

It is tempting to infer from the grid a 'natural' development path towards the top right of the grid ('Radically New'), which the collective perceptions of all partners should follow. But words such as 'should' have no place in the language of those who value difference, and although we believe 'Radically New' is an interesting and important box for many enterprises, and will devote much of this book to discussing it, we do not say it is the goal towards which all relationships should attempt to move, irrespective of their 'context': their environments and objectives.

It would be wrong, for example, if relationships between air-traffic controllers or nuclear power station operators were in any box other than 'Command and Control', and it can also be argued that the stage an industry or area of activity is at in its life-cycle (emergent, mature or declining) should be taken into account when selecting the appropriate box for its relationships.

However, although one can make few generally applicable judgements about the merits or otherwise of particular boxes, it seems clear to us that the 'context' of the modern world is moving in a direction that favours valuing difference (see Figure 2.2).

If asked to locate the modern management debates on Figure 2.2, most people would have little hesitation in saying they strad-dled the line dividing the 'Managing Difference' from the 'Valuing Difference' columns. The words in the middle column probably fit the language of modern management best, but the momentum is to the right. The words on the left seem inappropriate for modern times.

Images of conflict bombard us from all sides nowadays. The newspapers and newscasts are full of accounts of fierce and sometimes violent battles between religious or racial groups; between those who want to build new roads and those who want to preserve the countryside; between those who want to export or hunt live animals and those who feel such practices are cruel and inhumane; between those who want to dump oil rigs and nuclear waste at sea, or test nuclear weapons, and those who object to such 'environmental delinquency'; between those who demand more and those who refuse to give it.

Minimizing Difference	Managing Difference	Valuing Difference
• Environment is reasonably stable	• Environment is fiercely competitive	• Environment is complex and constantly changing
• Rate of change is stable	• Rate of change is accelerating	• Rate of change is discontinuous
• Resources are plentiful	• Resources are scarce	• Resources are threatened, and must be sustained
• External control is slight or non-existent	• External control is very tight	• External control is exercised through commitment
• Few significant stakeholder groups	• Several significant external stakeholder groups (customers, suppliers, neighbours, etc.)	• Numerous significant external stakeholder groups

Source: Tom Boydell

Figure 2.2   Context and difference

In most organizations and most societies it has gone beyond the stage when a reasonable strategy for managing difference is to try to minimize it. There is too much difference about now; we can no longer escape or ignore the demands of others to be heard. In free societies and open organizations, it is no longer possible to silence the cacophony of voices, views, values and beliefs. We are obliged by the spirit of our time (the *Zeitgeist*) to abandon all fundamentalism and accept the fact that people perceive reality in different ways, and that there is no single view about what should be done which all interested parties will agree to.

In other words, the modern environment, for the time being at any rate, is shifting towards a position where we will all be required to accept difference, and where those who can make a virtue of necessity and value difference will acquire a significant competitive advantage.

This obliges us to look at difference differently – to accept that it is OK to have a different view, and that differences, far from being constraints on strategy, are integral parts of the context within which strategy is formulated. After all, notwithstanding all the talk about the need for personal transformation before corporate transformation, it is much easier to change the objectives of a partnership than the nature of the partners.

One can never identify the best box without reference to the context, but one can say that the *Zeitgeist* imparts eastward momentum across the grid. Each perception has its appropriate contexts, but these days organizations are being obliged, by the context, to enter into more and more relationships where power is widely distributed, and where it is thus necessary to tolerate or value difference. It is not that the boxes on the right are 'better' or 'more modern' than those on the left; it is that organizations are entering relationships where the approaches of the left-hand boxes do not work.

In other words, we see 'Radically New' as a special place where the exigencies of the future are fully confronted. We cannot say any one box is the 'right' box, but we can say that in a pluralist age, when creativity seems both more desirable and less easy to find, effective relationships are those in which action is based on dialogue and the search for common ground, rather than on persuasion and the search for consensus.

The only general prescription offered by the grid is that we should be wary of prescribing. Its value lies in its ability to map the relationship space, and so allow partners to locate themselves – to understand where they are now and to see what options are open to them, should they decide that movement is necessary if they want to achieve their objectives.

Let us now explore the 'partnership spaces' delineated by the attitude to difference, and the collective ambition variables by briefly describing the grid's six boxes.

 ### 'Command and Control'

A widely held view is that the source of most of the problems encountered in relationships (including business partnerships and alliances), from the trivial to the life-threatening, is differences between the partners. This belief naturally leads to the

emergence of strategies aimed at eliminating, or at any rate minimizing, differences in objectives, processes, values and behaviour, typically by constructing common standards and rules, and
requiring all parties to the relationship to comply with them.

In these circumstances, the partnering relationship is formal
and largely based on negotiated contractual agreements. There is
a belief that every contingency can and should be planned for in
advance, in the light of the experiences of previous partnerships.
Thus, in 'command and control' partnerships, time must be
devoted to pre-contractual preparation, to ensure the partnership is 'set up right' in the first place.

It is in the nature of such a relationship that one partner,
invariably the largest, takes charge of drafting these rules. Also,
because the partnership is just a vehicle for completing a particular transaction, and so consists of little more than a mutual,
largely formal, exchange of resources, competencies or whatever
form a particular bargain takes, the relationship is generally seen
as short-term.

It follows from this that the characteristics of partnerships of
this kind are usually fairly accurate reflections of the characteristics of the dominant partner.

Appropriate context
'Command and control' strategies for minimizing differences are
the natural choice for relatively hierarchical organizations, and
are the 'natural' consequence when there is a significant imbal-
ance of power between partners. That they can work well and are
not inherently fragile is shown by the success and durability of
the Japanese *keiretsu* system, where a dominant central firm
orchestrates the activities of smaller suppliers and subcontractors.

The adoption of a 'command and control' style can also
improve the performance of a partnership that begins in another box. The relationship between a British healthcare trust and
one of its purchasers we studied in our research was fraught
with conflict after the organizational restructuring that brought
the partnership into being, but things improved visibly when the
partners began to focus on their contractual obligations. The
partners realized that their original, tacit assumptions about the

kind of partnership they were entering into were derived from an inaccurate perception of the new partnering context.

'Command and control' is suitable for partnerships that are not unduly ambitious, and where the partnership rationale can be construed as defensive. A hallmark of a defensive partnership is the effort put into planning and preparation. A number of those involved in a joint venture between two construction companies of much the same size attributed its success to the thoroughness of the formal and legal preparation.

Problems and weaknesses

One problem with such partnerships is that they always assume there is one *right view* (the dominant partner's), which must be policed, and policing is very expensive. The cost of 'policing' increases with the unpredictability of the environment, and puts 'command and control' partnerships at a serious disadvantage in turbulent environments.

Another problem is that the exercise of *force majeure* that shapes such partnerships frequently results in apportionments of reward that junior partners feel are unfair. Thus conflict is endemic in 'command and control' partnerships, and much time and energy must be devoted to managing its effects.

A third weakness is that the transactions for which this kind of partnership is the vehicle are between the top management teams, rather than whole organizations, so only a few senior people have a complete picture of what is going on. This and the use of *force majeure* are not conducive to the argument and mutual exploration that are the main engines of creative co-operation.

The high financial risks associated with a joint construction project in the Far East encouraged the lead contractor and largest partner to seek a high degree of control. This led to conflict, and thence to litigation reminiscent of the lengthy and very expensive legal squabbles that broke out between the builders and owners of the Channel Tunnel.

There are other ways in which the adoption of the 'command and control' approach can poison relationships. The restructuring of a major charity formally separated its two operating divisions. To reflect the changed relationship, the managers of one division spent six months drafting a contract with another, and so added emotional distance to the new structural distance.

A good example of how the 'command and control' strategy, taken to its extreme, can destroy a partnership is the case of the putative 'partnership' between an English local authority and the trade unions representing its employees. Management simply by-passed the unions, thus marginalizing them and effectively pushing the relationship 'off the map'.

 &

'Hearts and Minds'

In this box, difference is minimized by a search for sameness and alignment, rather than by an imposed, external structure. The assumption is that if all partners think and feel alike and share a basic culture, they will be able to work together in harmony and produce mutually beneficial outcomes.

Whenever people talk of a need for all partners to 'sing from the same hymn-sheet', they are advocating the 'hearts and minds' approach.

Organizations that believe the articulation of shared visions is the way to win the commitment of their own employees tend to bring the same philosophy to the partnerships they join. An example of such a philosophy, and the problems it can cause when contexts change and present new challenges, is provided by developments at the Mondragón community of industrial co-operatives in the Basque country, in northern Spain (see page 152).

Appropriate context
This assiduous synthesis of a shared culture was seen by many who participated in our research – particularly by those whose previous partnering experience had been marked by conflict or confrontation – as the 'ideal' approach.

The policy of the 'virtual corporation' of consultants was to work only with people who shared the same values. The success of the business shows such 'hearts and minds' relationships can work well.

Some interviewees from the construction companies that worked well together under a carefully planned 'command and control' relationship also attributed the joint venture's success to similarities in 'size and culture'. This shows how different but compatible perceptions of the same relationship can often co-exist. In this case, the relationship was clearly in the 'Avoid Difference' part of the grid, but some parties to the partnership harboured more ambitious visions about the future of the relationship than others.

Examples of how attractive a 'hearts and minds' relationship can seem to those who are not in one were provided by respondents in the French electronics firm, who attributed their failure to forge a good relationship with a US software firm to their very different 'personalities', and how people in the healthcare partnership which improved when it switched to 'command and control' (see above) yearned for 'hearts and minds': they felt it was the sort of relationship they had enjoyed before the restructuring, when they and the purchasers were both members of the same organization. It was the contrast between the previous cultural unity and the abrupt cultural divergence that made it so hard for many of them to make sense of and deal with the bitter conflicts the new relationship ignited.

The two divisions of the charity mentioned above also mourned the loss of a shared culture. Indeed, one division saw the prolonged gestation of its contract with the other, which marked the switch to 'command and control', as adding insult to the injury of cultural exile.

Ambitious partnerships between similar partners will tend to find their way to this box, and it is the place where almost all relationships between acquirer and acquired companies end up. It is therefore a perfectly logical box to choose if an acquisition is preferable but impossible (for regulatory or other reasons).

Problems and weaknesses
It is not clear from our research that the 'hearts and minds' relationship always delivers its alleged benefits, and there is some evidence to the contrary.

One problem with this approach to minimizing difference is that while 'command and control' openly outlaws difference, 'hearts and minds' often just papers over the cracks, so the tyranny of power is replaced by the tyranny of culture. Conflict goes underground, and because it ceases to exist officially in the 'culturally re-engineered' relationship, no attempt is made to manage it.

Another problem with the 'hearts and minds' approach is that it contains a logical flaw (which we will explore in more detail in Chapter 6) that can have serious practical consequences. Unlike 'command and control', it takes an ambitious, long-term view of the relationship, and is thus ready to invest effort and resources in establishing and maintaining it. But most of the effort goes into minimizing the very quality, difference, that offers the partnership its best chance of prospering in the long term.

It is very hard to attribute partnership failures directly to the 'hearts and minds' philosophy, because its weaknesses tend to be obscured by the 'cultural homogenization' it seeks, and often achieves. Its flaws take the form of lost opportunities, and may show up in general feelings of dissatisfaction people find hard to explain, or suspicions that the partnership could have worked better. Most of the mavericks and the dissidents are silenced or ejected during the homogenization process, so the sub-optimal result is seldom officially recognized.

But if, as we suggested above, post-acquisition relationships between acquirer and acquired are usually of the 'hearts and minds' type, indirect evidence of the flaws in this approach can be found in the performance of acquisitions. A study by Michael Porter (1987) of 33 large, acquisitive firms found that most had sold many more companies than they had kept, and that the most successful acquisitions were those in the same industry, where differences were lower at the outset.

Most researchers who have tried to explain the generally poor performance of acquisitions in cultural terms have concluded that the problem is an inadequate homogenization of cultures. In our view, it is more likely that the opposite is the case, and the reason acquisitions so frequently fail to deliver the expected added value is that acquiring firms are unwilling to tolerate, let alone value, the differences that are the source of the value they seek.

'Arm's Length'

There will always be a tendency for collective perceptions of a partnership to move to an adjacent box on the grid, as the perceivers' views of and responses to difference change and develop.

We have already seen how a partnership that aspires to a 'hearts and minds' approach can fail to achieve the necessary cultural fusion and, still yearning for minimal difference, can end up in the 'Command and Control' box.

In the same way, 'command and control' behaviour can mutate into 'arm's length' behaviour when the attitude to difference becomes less uncompromising. Indeed, this is in a way an inevitable step when no partner is dominant and when the relationship must continue for any length of time. It is only possible to suppress differences for a while. Sooner or later they emerge, and if the partnership is to survive, they must be tolerated.

In the 'arm's length' relationship, risk is managed by 'agreeing to differ', careful planning and relatively formal procedures for settling disputes. Good communication, including periodic checks on understanding, are seen as absolutely vital in such partnerships. Flexibility is deemed valuable, as long as it does not require the loss of too much ground or identity. The relationship tends to be distant and tinged with mild mutual suspicion.

As is the case in all relationships, the rationales for which are largely defensive and relatively unambiguous, there is a temporary quality to 'arm's length' partnerships. They continue as long as the expected mutual benefits materialize, but partners reserve the moral as well as the legal right to withdraw at their convenience or seek other partners, if the relationship gets into difficulties.

Appropriate context

Such partnerships remain regulated, and dependent on external controls and structures, but are less dependent on enforcing uniformity. Firms who prefer the 'command and control' approach may realize that if they want to work with foreign partners, for example, they may have to live with a little strangeness.

Interviewees at the European electronics firm we studied said they had learned not to rush into formal contracts, for fear of creating loop-holes that could be exploited by their subcontractors and partners. They felt that because they could not control or entirely trust their partners, they needed to be free to respond flexibly to every contingency.

Similarly, the special projects division of the British civil engineering firm has found it is impossible to anticipate all contingencies when dealing with foreign partners; and without regular meetings to check consensus, obscure cultural nuances can cause operational misunderstandings and other problems.

Problems and weaknesses

The main weakness of the 'arm's length' relationship is that it is defensive and lacks much ambition. Partners tolerate each other's 'idiosyncrasies', but make little effort to establish mutual trust. This probably means that such relationships fail to exploit their full potential, although for obvious reasons this is hard to prove in particular cases.

This sense of untapped potential was apparent in the case of two European computer firms who were in the habit of piggybacking each other for marketing purposes, and had found ways to be 'civilized', despite the fact that 'We don't trust them an inch.'

The relationship we studied between a European computer firm and an English software firm was similarly constrained. They delivered into each other's systems, but had made no attempt to create an integrated interface because, as one respondent put it: 'It's important not to concede too much ground.'

It may be argued that unexploited potential is not a flaw in an 'arm's length' relationship if the partners had no desire to exploit it. This is a reasonable argument, if one assumes the objectives of the partnership are given at the outset and are immutable thereafter. But if there is untapped potential in an 'arm's length' partnership that could be released if the partners were more ambitious and if they valued rather than tolerated difference, it seems reasonable to suggest there is a flaw in the objective, if not in the relationship.

'Do and Review'

A relationship that tolerates difference but takes a longer-term view than that of a temporary, 'arm's length' partnership needs more committed and trusting partners. A 'do and review' partnership extends the 'arm's length' approach's emphasis on planning and process design from the operational to the strategic aspects of the relationship.

All partners accept that the objectives are multi-dimensional and must change to adapt to new opportunities and threats. There is an ethic of collaboration and co-operation, an assumption that the partnership is long-term, and a focus on learning and the continuous improvement of the partnership's processes and systems.

The provisional qualities of the 'arm's length' relationship are less evident in 'do and review' partnerships. There is a sense of sharing a future as well as a present. Such relationships still move step by step, and from project to project, but the purpose of the reviews following each step is to learn how to partner better, rather than to decide whether the partnership is worth continuing with.

Appropriate context

Partners in this box describe their relationships as 'trusting', and are willing to go out of their way to cement trust. Those directly involved in the partnership all have a clear picture of what is going on.

This is quite a popular box. Our research produced several examples of 'do and review' relationships, one feature of which is the effort partners made to understand each other's positions.

The European electronics firm has a Partnership and Alliances Director who regularly visits established partners to discuss changing market needs and identify new opportunities.

Before drawing up its strategic plan, the UK local authority's planning department held a series of workshops to seek the views of all employees, and then modified its objectives in the light of the findings.

Although generally more comfortable in 'command and control' or 'arm's length' relationships, the UK construction group helped a small local contractor with a technical problem, so saving him the expense of a consultant engineer. (This suggests that although a company may be most comfortable in one particular box, there exists in most partnerships the potential for very different kinds of relationships.)

A long-term partnership between a European computer group and a US software firm runs a permanent partnership conference on *Lotus Notes*, to facilitate joint learning and generate rapid feedback about how each of the partners think joint projects are progressing.

The strong project orientation of 'do and review' relationships was also evident in the 'virtual corporation' of consultants, which holds regular meetings to reflect on the success, or otherwise, of projects and learn how to work better together in the future.

Problems and weaknesses

The aims of 'do and review' partnerships can be prodigious, but are seldom radical. The step-by-step rhythm of 'do and review' relationships shows that the joint quest is for incremental rather than transformational achievement.

This suggests that although this is a pretty good box to occupy in many ways, the problem of untapped potential discussed in 'arm's length' relationships is only partially solved, and much more could be achieved if partners valued rather than merely tolerated difference.

In other words, ambition is multi-dimensional, and although 'do and review' relationships are ambitious about the durability of the relationship (how long they want it to last), there is a lack of depth to their ambition. The purpose of the efforts to achieve mutual understanding is to make the relationship work efficiently, not to explore the maximum potential of the association.

Here again, one can suggest there is a flaw in the objective, if not in the relationship itself.

'Gridlock'

This is perhaps the most challenging of all the boxes on the grid, because it contains what appear to be strong internal contradictions. Its location defines it as lacking ambition, but as actively seeking to work with differences, rather than against them. Notwithstanding Scott Fitzgerald's opinion that 'The test of first rate intelligence is to hold two opposing ideas in mind, and still have the ability to function,' these two attitudes are hard to reconcile in practice.

When difference is seen as a valuable resource, two things can happen: the creative potential can be realized, in which case there will be a strong tendency for the relationship to adopt a more ambitious purpose; or it can fail to materialize (because of conflict, bad management or incompatible ideas about the appropriate balance of power), and partners will become less convinced of the value of difference and be inclined to move to the left of the grid.

We have found that there is a great deal of inertia in this box, however. Merely seeing the positive potential and recognizing the need to respect and work with a multiplicity of views and agendas does not mean you know what to do. These partnerships are so constrained by their extreme political instability that they often feel incapable of acting, for fear of sinking the boat. Partners become obsessed with an internal positioning process that prevents them from identifying, let alone working on, the one thing that can break the gridlock – a mutually compelling joint project.

'Gridlock' is a response to situations in which power is widely distributed. It is characterized by compromise and efforts to keep the peace and ensure no one 'loses face'. Its effect is to add to the fragmented power a fragmented purpose, and to focus the attention on power and face-saving rather than the task at hand. People in 'gridlock' are so preoccupied with the relationship itself that they forget what it is for.

Appropriate context

The appropriateness or otherwise of this approach is directly related to the level of instability in the system, and to the fear of doing anything to upset the delicate balance. For example, if the instability is such that any movement by any partner might blow the whole thing sky high, this box might be preferable to boxes to the left of it, particularly if the number of parties involved is large and the configuration is complex.

A 'gridlock' perspective is unlikely to be shared by all the constituencies in the partnership, however, and the extent to which partners are content with this box will often have more to do with their nervousness about losing their autonomy than with an objective assessment of the system's fragility.

Our experience suggests that the ways partners perceive their contexts are very deeply ingrained in their general outlooks, including the differences they see, and that whether partners see themselves in the 'Gridlock' or the more creative 'Radically New' box depends on the lens they are looking through when making the judgement.

To be in 'gridlock' is to be Damocles, confronted by a feast of obscure opportunities while consumed by fear.

Problems and weaknesses

As already indicated, the problems and weaknesses of 'gridlock' are largely superficial. The more partners look at the problems, the more they appear to be part of the relationship itself. Those who see themselves in this box are likely to be confined to defensive and preventive behaviour against their will or better judgement.

The constraints that frustrate 'gridlocked' partners may take the form of rules, regulations, group strategy, environmental factors, the marketplace or their prejudices. It is unlikely that all partners would be content to remain in 'gridlock' and deny themselves and each other a chance to capture the value they see in their differences, particularly as the alternative must lead to the rebellion, retreat or apathy of some if not all the parties.

 ### 'Radically New'

When differences of all kinds are not only valued but also actively explored, partners begin to see their relationship as, if not yet a solution, at least a place where a solution might be found to the most pressing problem of all – the need for organizations to change themselves utterly to cope with a turbulent present and an unpredictable future.

In these circumstances the partnership becomes not merely an adjunct to each partner's ways of being, but an integral part of their essence. Difference is valued, and the perspectives of everyone in the partnering organizations contribute to and help to define the relationship. Rather than seeking a shared vision of the future, the partners try to construct a picture of their shared present by exploring a multiplicity of views and values.

Partners cease to try to change or 'convert' each other (that would take them back to 'hearts and minds'), and instead embark on a joint search for 'common ground' on which, despite their differences (or because of them), there are possibilities for joint action.

The partnership is never defined – it is encouraged to emerge from the day-to-day experience of working together. All the feelings of separateness that made 'gridlock' so uncomfortable and frustrating are abandoned, and a shared sense of destiny comes to dominate the outlook of all those involved.

'Radically New' is, in a way, the ultimate box: the place where difference is valued so much and partnering sights are set so high that the creative potential of partnering is maximized.

Such thoroughgoing partnerships remain rare, but our research provided two examples of relationships that incorporated some of the principles of 'radically new', if not yet the full-blown reality.

The overseas division of a charity convened a three-day local partners' forum in Kenya, where local groups competing for its resources were asked to set the agenda and to suggest changes to the charity's way of doing business.

To promote environmental regeneration, the planning department of the district council created a 'space' in which everyone's views and concerns were heard by everyone else. This obliged councillors, officers and local community groups to find new ways of working together.

Appropriate context
A 'radically new' relationship is necessary when both power and knowledge are so widely distributed between the partners that no other kind of relationship can work. It may be appropriate in other contexts, too, where those with power recognize that the full creative potential of the partnership they seek to tap will not be realized until they surrender their power.

Problems and weaknesses
A respect for difference can lead to inaction, because nothing will be clear, nothing will be resolved, and all dialogue will end in bland compromises and agreements to differ.

'Radically new' is a very risky approach, because it requires partners to exchange their traditional identities for a new collective identity. They have to put their fates in the hands of others, and if the partnership fails, it may be hard for the partners to retrieve their old identities.

Moreover, because it is an emergent rather than a purposeful fusion of beings, 'radically new' can creep up on you. You may not be aware that the growing intimacy of the partnership has eroded your organization's sense of identity until it is too late to halt the process, should you wish to do so. The tendency to move up the Partnering Grid as trust develops, and to become more collectively ambitious, weakens the cultural 'glue' that binds people to their organizations. Loyalty and commitment can seep away from the individual partners and become vested in the partnership.

Summary

The Partnership Grid reveals the individual perceptions of those involved in a partnership, so by overlaying individual perceptions, a collective picture can be built up of the positions on the grid of all partner organizations, and thus of the partnership itself.

Each particular partnership is, of course, extremely complex, because it consists of numerous individual perceptions that differ widely, both between and within partner organizations. For example, the way the financial controller of one partner organization perceives the partnership may be much closer to the way his or her opposite number in the other organization perceives it than to the way his or her own Human Resources colleagues do.

The grid's diagnostic power lies in its ability to reduce all these perceptions to what we (and many of those who have used the Partnering Grid as a diagnostic tool) believe are the two most important dimensions of partnering, the dimensions that, when combined, illuminate the unspoken assumptions about what partnership in general and this particular partnership mean.

Sometimes the diagnosis will reveal that all is well and that the partnership is perceived in ways that are appropriate for its environment and objectives. But the decision to do the diagnosis in the first place means that, in most cases, it will give substance to suspicions that something is wrong, and indicate a need for movement in the grid.

We will discuss how individuals and organizations move around the Partnering Grid in search of 'fit' in Chapter 4. Before that, we want to corroborate the grid in two ways.

First, we invite readers to 'experiment' with it in their own organizations or partnerships by plotting their perceptions and those of their colleagues or partners with the help of a condensed version of our partnering software in Appendix A.

Second, we shall describe in Chapter 3 some of the 'tools for thought' that contributed to the development of the grid.

Story from the front: a tale of two partnerships

The former executive of a large multinational company we are not at liberty to name shared with us his reflections on two large partnerships he was intimately involved with, using the grid as the framework for his comments:

We never used the grid, but it would have been very useful with our mergers and acquisitions, especially the idea that views of difference differ. The only attitude we had was avoidance, or toleration, of difference – most of our strategy was bottom left ['Command and Control'].

There was some co-operation, collaboration and sharing views, but mostly for the purpose of preventing negatives.

I was involved in the early stages with two major alliances. In both cases we would have avoided a partnership if it had been possible; we were succumbing to the inevitable. We would have preferred to grow ourselves, in all markets. If we could not do that, we would have preferred to buy companies outright, so partnering was really the third best option.

The first partner didn't like the idea at all; it was forced into it by government. And the other would not have agreed to do it if they had not needed our cash. Our original plan was to buy it outright, but we had to settle for a minority stake. Our culture was very centrist; we preferred to run everything from our head office.

That changed later; we learned how to do it. The franchising programme (where we have effectively loaned our brand to some smaller companies) would not have been considered in the old days, but it has become more acceptable now. The franchises worked very well, better than the alliances, because we could forget about them. With alliances, the wheels are spinning all the time.

Individuals are moving up the grid and to the right, because continuous exposure forces them to recognize that 'these guys are better than us at some things'. We realized, for example, that our US partner was much better at operational planning, whereas we were better at the 'big picture'. They could operate larger networks, with far more customers, and some of our operations people had a lot of exposure to that.

It was because the US style is focused on quarterly results; people are set short-term targets. The British style is less short-term focused, and that is a weakness and a strength. It means we're not so good at planning, but also that we're more flexible, and we see the big picture more clearly. While they stuck rigidly to plan, we were willing to throw the plan away for the right reasons. We are more used to not being planned.

Many of our procedures were learned from our US partner; they are much better at operating large sites. There were a lot of other operational things we could have learned from them, had the partnership lasted.

The company as a whole is staying in the bottom left of the grid, but some individuals see things differently. There are long lags and huge dampers on getting that to the company, however. It may learn from individuals eventually, but it will take a long time.

The real obstacle is the law. It's a regulated industry, and the degree of control you have is always limited.

The idea that you can have partnership and no control – that you can get a high degree of partnership with a low level of legal involvement – was part of the original vision, but it needed both companies to move significantly to the middle and top right of the grid.

Some early discussions seemed quite promising. We got senior officers from both companies locked away, and discussed what might be possible. It got to a position where the long-term perspective was that we should operate as one company, to all intents and purposes. But if people are not seeing each other every week, such visions fade and anything that goes wrong is immediately seen as a conspiracy rather than a cock-up. Trust diminishes exponentially if you don't see people.

We needed a greater feeling of common purpose within the two companies. For most people, the primary allegiance was to the company; the partnership was secondary. We felt the other way round, but we were the exceptions.

The partnership degenerated to a minimum 'maintenance' level with just enough contact to keep the business relationship going.

It was a great pity. I gave two years of my life to it, and I still think the potential benefits were huge.

The distancing began way before we sold the shares. It began with a difference of opinion between the CEOs on further cash injections. Their position was: 'Trust us to sort it out, but we need more cash.' We switched from being a white to a black knight when our CEO refused to subscribe to a rights issue. That seemed like a betrayal to them – they felt right through the company that they had been shafted.

The other partner didn't want us, but their government wanted a trade investor, and we were seen as the least bad option. Things changed when a new CEO took over and brought in a new management team. They wanted a joint service agreement [JSA], and we acquired a common enemy in the government, and became closer. But it was hard to be really close when there was so little common office time. (The first thing we did, with both alliances, was to establish regular e-mail contact.)

The relationship has had its ups and downs, but it was always a much more 'instrumental' partnership than the one with the US company. Both sides were getting something out of it. They didn't feel we were the dominant partner, so the conversations were between grown-ups. But it was much shallower than the US relationship; there is little co-operation beyond the JSA, and we were all too busy to think seriously about how it might be deepened.

An important issue, when choosing your partners, is how much you can trust them. We spoke to most of the major companies in our sector. Some had partners already, but said they would drop them for us – that makes you wonder how trustworthy they are. The trust you get is the trust you earn.

Humour plays an important part in a bi-cultural partnership. Americans often see the British sense of humour as underhand and cynical. At the beginning of the relationship with the US company, some of the Americans took exception to my jokes, but they learned to make allowances for me. That is an important step: learning to make allowances for cultural gaffes. Humour can go horribly wrong across cultures.

You also have to deal with intra-company differences between departmental cultures. That is a big issue if a company wants to move to the top right of the partnering grid. We had often been very departmentalized, when different departments insist on sticking to procedures laid down for the relationship, but at other periods there has been a lot of rule-breaking, risk-taking and opening up according to the Japanese 'open kimono' principle.

It would be very useful to develop a mechanism for moving in the grid; finding new ways to initiate movement. In my view, the way to move is to have lots of face-to-face meetings, so people have more opportunities to feel 'They're just like us,' or 'They're different, but the difference is valuable.' It is like unilateral disarmament. Don't wait until the company says it is OK to share information – do it now. It is very difficult, however, because people have to take personal risks, and then convince the company after the event.

We were good in short periods of crisis when everyone has to do anything and people have to trust each other. We had a few crises. They were great fun and lasted for quite a while. The work was managed differently. There was much more emphasis on customer service, and management was very open with staff and other areas; the whole company was more open. There was a lot of risk-taking and rule-breaking.

Summary

Since all partnerships are compromises, partners should spend less time trying to harmonize and align, and more time trying to understand each other.

Our research was designed to help partners understand each other and develop trust by working together.

Partnerships can be plotted on a matrix relating ambition to view of difference, which we call the Partnering Grid. Each box has distinctive characteristics, and each is better suited to certain contexts than others.

Grid positions describe the perceptions of individual partners. A collective picture of the whole partnership can be built by overlaying these individual perceptions.

References

Porter, M. (1987) 'From competitive advantage to corporate strategy', *Harvard Business Review*, May/June.

3 The origins of the grid

The idea of the Partnering Grid we described in Chapter 2 was inspired by our research and various 'tools for thought' that we have found useful when working with the management problems confronting large business enterprises in a complex and turbulent world.

However, just as each solution carries within it the seeds of the next generation of problems, these thought tools answer some questions while begging others. In our work with the Partnering Grid we have addressed this next generation of questions, but we recognize we have probably also posed a new set of questions and opened up new avenues of exploration and discovery.

In this chapter we shall briefly describe some of these tools, and explain how they have shaped our thinking and continue to influence the development of our work with the Partnering Grid. The grid is, in a way, a representation of these concepts, ideas and theories, so readers who feel short of time can skip this chapter without losing track of the argument. But although none of these ideas are difficult, some are unfamiliar by the standards of the modern management discourse, so it is worth taking the time to scan what follows, in order to acclimatize the mind for the journey ahead.

The ideas fall into three main categories:

1   ideas about organizational learning
2   ideas about organizational activity
3   ideas about seeing and knowing.

New tools for thought are desperately needed in a world that is becoming so saturated in difference (in how people behave, what they believe in, and how they expect things to develop) and so 'connected' (through the communications explosion and the development of new distributed organizational structures) that the old tools that we used to make sense of things have started to lose much of their relevance.

Generally speaking, these old tools for thought were based on empirical, rational, so-called 'modernist' approaches which make certain, often implicit, assumptions about the way things are. They assume, for example, that there is always a single correct answer to a problem that can be deduced by logic and reason from a set of unambiguous facts. There are an enormous number of problems that are 'soluble' in this way, but one of the most distinctive characteristics of the modern world is the enormous growth in the number of problems (those relating to culture, language and values, for example) that are simply insoluble by the modernist approach.

Business is not immune to this epidemic of inherently complex problems, as many managers know only too well. Old solutions often do not work as they used to, and even when they do, they have other unexpected and unwelcome consequences. Part of the problem is that the old linear approach to problem-solving relied on a centralized system of power and authority that is disappearing in the age of partnership enterprise.

Differences can no longer be casually dismissed with the wave of an autocratic hand. Business managers and leaders need to arm themselves with new ideas, frameworks, concepts and ways of understanding that will enable them to live with all the difference they have spent their working lives trying hard to eradicate. To manage effectively in a world where difference is endemic and ineradicable, they must adopt what philosophers call a 'postmodernist' view, recognizing that the 'rightness' or 'wrongness' of anything is in the eye of the beholder, and turning 'either/or' into 'both/and'.

We will argue in this chapter that although modern management thinking is beginning to tackle the problem of difference and ambiguity, it is doing so within the conventional 'modernist' framework that will prove incapable of accommodating the deep shifts of outlook that are needed before much progress can be made.

The flaw in the conventional framework is that it approaches relationship issues as if they were technical problems, and assumes that there is only one 'right' way for the parties in the relationship to behave. This establishes an ideal form or nature for the relationship that takes little or no account of the actual conditions of the relationship, as perceived by the parties, and precludes the search for other relationships that are significantly different from the ideal. Any undesirable outcomes of attempts to improve relationships so that they become more like the ideal can be attributed to the failure of the individuals involved to behave 'properly'. In other words, it is assumed that all relationship problems are the result of the inability or refusal of individuals to behave in ways required by the ideal relationship.

If the conventional modernist approach cannot handle all the complexity and ambiguity inherent in the alliance enterprise, what can? Where should we look for these postmodernist ideas that can bring some order to the messiness of modern business relationships without recourse to the central organizing and orchestrating power that has served us well in the past but is now so often beyond our reach?

Organizational learning

The inspiration of the three columns of the Partnering Grid described in Chapter 2 was the classification of 'learning types' proposed by Tom Boydell, Mike Pedler and John Burgoyne of the Learning Company Project, (Pedler et al., 1991).

This provided a way of thinking about organizational learning that was distinct from individual learning, while at the same time less tainted by the organization and its processes than most models of organizational learning. All three 'types of learning' occur within organizations, and each is appropriate in certain situations and circumstances. Figure 3.1 describes the types of learning, and includes some brief comments on their roles and weaknesses.

Implementing (doing things well)

Here, the focus is on implementing what is already agreed, on the resources involved, and on operating associated processes efficiently. In a partnership 'Implementing learning' (*Ia*) is concerned with the content of the partnership (the skills and resources being exchanged). The learning is linear, and based on exchanges of

Type	Description	Danger/weakness
I^a – Implementing (habit)	• Does things well • Matches best current practice consistently and reliably • Does not respond to changes in environment	• Gets left behind; becomes rigid, inward-looking, unresponsive to change; standards slip due to lack of systematic improvement procedure; emphasis on routine and obedience leads to high costs
I^b – Improving (asserting)	• Does things better • Continuous improvement through systematic feedback and reflection; responds to changes by adapting	• Tampering leads to instability; limited improvements within existing boundaries • Emphasis on economic efficiency leads to high costs elsewhere (e.g., social, environmental)
I^c – Integrating (mutuality)	• Does better things • Acknowledges multiple stakeholder interests and complexity through dialogue and collective interpretation • Supports 'virtual organizing' and 'just-in-time' alliances • Co-creates its environment	• Confusion over identity • Soggy compromise rather than radical breakthrough • Lapsing into discursive inaction

Source: The Learning Company Project

Figure 3.1   Types of organizational learning

ideas and operating experience between people with similar out-looks and cultural affiliations. Perceptions of how learning should proceed are based on what the parties already know or possess and can therefore teach or give each other.

The main weakness of *Ia* learning is that it is not responsive to what goes on outside the learning situation, and for this rea-son what is learned tends to become obsolete before it is fully digested.

Improving (doing things better)

The focus here is on improving 'processes' through feedback and reflection. The emphasis is on learning to do things as well as they can possibly be done, rather than on just doing them well enough. 'Improving learning' (*Ib*) produces continuous improve-ment (what the Japanese call *kaizen*). Content is less important than process, and enterprises are seen as consisting of processes rather than assets. People are more concerned with what others do than with what they possess, and learning is cyclical rather than linear.

The main weaknesses of *Ib* learning are that it is unstable in the sense that what is learned today may have to be unlearned tomorrow; improvement is constrained within relatively narrow boundaries and the feedback and reflection on which it feeds is exclusively focused on the processes concerned, and takes no account of the 'wider picture', or of what economists call 'exter-nalities', such as social and environmental issues.

Integrating (doing better things)

The focus here is on integrating knowledge and finding better things to do, as opposed to finding ways to do things better. Innovation and creativity are sought through dialogue and a sys-tems-based approach to problem-solving, and context is all-important. 'Integrating learning' (*Ic*) seeks to understand why things are done in the ways they are done, and thus welcomes different values and perspectives. Dialogue, not feedback, is the main engine of learning, and enterprise potential is seen in terms not of what others have or do, but of who they are.

The main weaknesses of *Ic* learning are that it tends to breed confusion, and can end up with compromise or ambiguity rather than true synthesis.

Summary

As we have said, and as our readers know full well, all three types of organizational learning go on more or less all the time, just as all three of the attitudes to difference in the Partnering Grid they inspired co-exist and together comprise the totality of the partnership. Each learning type and each attitude to difference has strengths and weaknesses, and each can strengthen or weaken the others.

Figure 3.2 maps the learning types onto the Partnering Grid, and reveals the correspondences between the *Is* of learning and the grid's three attitudes to difference in a partnership context.

As Figure 3.2 suggests, the learning model associated with *Ia* and the left-hand column of the grid can be characterized as 'linear'; the learning model associated with *Ib* and the grid's middle column can be characterized as 'cyclical', and the model associ-

Learning Focus	Implementing	Improving	Integrating
Notion of partnering	• What? = transaction • Value of different possessions	• How? = business process • Value of different processes	• Why? = identity • Value of different values
Learning from partner	• Linear: exchange	• Cyclical: review in the light of experience	• Dialogue: mutual causality
Partnering affects ...	• What we have	• What we do	• Who we are
View of Difference	Avoid	Tolerate	Value

Figure 3.2   Learning in partnerships

ated with *Ic* and the right-hand column can be characterized as 'dialogue'.

The challenge to partnerships lies in assessing the extent to which their learning approaches fit the type of outcomes they wish to achieve. Given the complexity and unpredictability of the contemporary environment, and the ambitious goals of many contemporary partnerships, we believe that generally speaking there is far too much *Ia* learning going on, and far too little *Ic* learning.

We hope that this book will inspire readers to talk about and experiment with *Ic* learning. (See Appendix C for descriptions of a number of practical ways to stimulate *Ic* learning.)

Organizational activity

Although all the recent enthusiasm for the so-called 'learning organization' might lead one to suppose otherwise, the fate of enterprises is determined by what they do, not by how or what they learn. Learning is important, but when all is said and done, it is merely a means to the end of effective action, and theories about how organizations 'learn' often tell us little about how they 'act'.

A major problem in a partnership enterprise is how to achieve coherent, collective action by a set of relatively autonomous actors. We therefore realized that if the Partnering Grid was to shed useful light on the performance of organizations, we needed a theory of 'collective action' as well as a theory of 'collective learning'.

One person who has been studying the link between learning and action is Bob Lewis, Professor of Knowledge Technology, Information Systems and Services at Lancaster University in the UK. He says that a useful way to think about collective action is to suppose that an individual's knowledge consists of a central, owned 'core' knowledge that equips him or her to act autonomously, surrounded by a ring of partial knowledge where he or she needs help to act.

As Figure 3.3 shows, when individuals gather into communities, their cores and rings of partial knowledge overlap, and in so doing often remove some of the deficiencies that prevent autonomous action. In this way, members enrich group knowledge by providing what Lewis calls 'scaffolding', which transforms segments of individual, partial knowledge into the whole group's core knowledge, thus enabling collective action.

We believe that these insights are fundamental to an understanding of the foundations that need to be in place before collective action can be effective. At present they are rarely recognized or developed, but they have been central to our thinking. The characteristics of these foundation stones are described below.

For this synergistic potential of a learning or working group to be realized, the communications system its members use must be

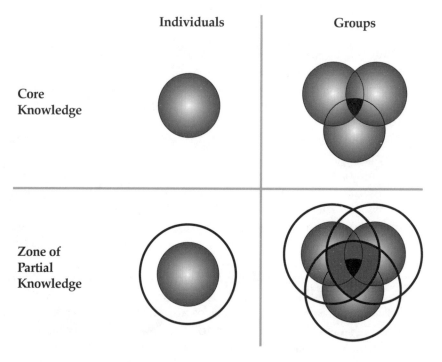

Source: Bob Lewis

Figure 3.3   Knowledge in community

capable of describing the core and approximate knowledge of each member, of facilitating a trade in knowledge, and of monitoring the core knowledge 'owned' by the group, as well as that 'owned' by individual members. This suggests that the design of a group's communications system helps determine not only how well its members communicate, but also the extent of its core knowledge, and thus the ability of each of its members to act autonomously.

The capacity for 'autonomous action' is important, because at certain stages of a collective endeavour the need will arise to switch between what we call 'participative activity', when the members work together to achieve a single common goal, and 'collaborative activity', when members help each other to achieve their own personal goals, and the common purpose is a complex, changing interplay between what is individually and collectively possible.

If acting together effectively requires periodic shifts from participative to collaborative activity and back again, we need a theory that makes sense of such phase transitions (and the shifts in expectations and power that accompany them) so that we can choose the most appropriate 'settings' for action and address the important question of 'media choice' to which we shall return in Chapter 7.

Moreover, because the transfer of the impetus for action from the few to the many is always difficult and problematic, the theory needs to provide some kind of framework that can help us understand why problems arise and see how to avoid them. Activity Theory (AT), which dates back to the Russian systems theories developed in the 1920s, fits the bill. It bears some of the marks of the obsolete political agenda for which it was designed, but its social and ecological perspectives on human activity distinguish it as a theory largely untainted by the subtle prejudice that makes it hard for modern systems theorists to think of systems without thinking of computers.

The general shape of AT is shown in Figure 3.4. It says that human beings ('subjects') are helped by such artefacts as language, conceptual frameworks, rules of dialogue, computers, etc. ('tools') to achieve objectives ('objects'), and are willing to accept

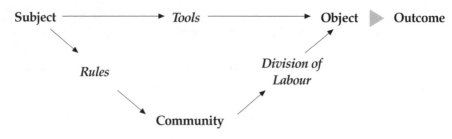

Source: Bob Lewis

Figure 3.4   Activity Theory

'rules' to work in communities, if they are seen to contribute to the achievement of the objectives. The rules AT theorists have in mind are the assumptions or 'mental models' individuals bring to collaboration. An important part of our argument is that unless these assumptions are rendered visible, collaboration will break down.

There are three 'levels' of activity in AT – activity, action and operation:

- **Activity** deals with the motive, needs, values and desires. It gives meaning to human processes, and since it involves high levels of ambiguity, it requires the richest possible forms of communication, such as face-to-face meetings.
- **Action** focuses on specific goals derived from the motive. It involves organizational planning and problem-solving, and can be done well enough through leaner communications media such as video-conferencing.
- **Operation** is practical, routine action, where there is no ambiguity. Simpler forms of communication such as e-mail and faxes are usually adequate here.

The framework is 'dynamic', in that human actions move between the three activity levels in response to 'frustrations' and 'contradictions'. If problems or inconsistencies arise at the operational level, for instance, the group may have to shift to the action level to resolve them. Similarly, problems that arise at the action level which cannot be resolved there go on the agenda for the next face-to-face meeting.

The key to the effectiveness of action is that the same group of people must act on all levels. Disjunction, for example as one small group sets vision and goals (activity level), and then hands over to another group to plan and implement (action and operation levels), breeds dysfunction.

This suggests that before all these three levels can be woven together to generate coherent collective action, two things are necessary: a recognition of the need for very widespread participation at each level, and the development of processes and procedures that permit activity-level work to take place within large and diverse groups.

Learning and acting on the grid

The three columns of the Partnering Grid accommodate and help to clarify the correspondences between AT's three levels of activity and the three types of learning identified by Tom Boydell, Mike Pedler and John Burgoyne.

Left-hand column ('Avoid Difference')

This is the domain of the *Ia* (implementing) type of learning and the 'operation' level of action. Both are based on habit and the unquestioning acceptance that 'this is the way things are done'. People who undertake or oversee operations may adopt a tolerant or even a positive attitude to difference in other situations and at other times, but they assume that for these operations 'the book' is God, and that any divergence from it will be counter-productive.

'The book' is immune to challenge, because of the characteristic concentration of power in the left-hand column. It is not that all activity in this column is inherently operational and all learning is inherently implementing; it is that, in this part of the grid, power is sufficiently concentrated to permit the confinement of all activity to this level, and all learning to this type.

In this way, concentrated power leads to the concentration of knowledge, and people participate in implementing the agendas of those with the power.

Middle column ('Tolerate Difference')

This is the domain of *Ib* learning (improving) and AT's 'action'. Both are concerned with improving and doing things better. The focus is on processes which consist of manageable chunks of more or less bounded actions. Here, the attitude to difference has to be more tolerant, because the parameters of actions cannot be 'set in stone'. When action can be improved (and 'the book' can always do with a rewrite), it is necessary to listen to those who question 'the book', because their ideas may help to improve it.

There is more ambiguity and turbulence here, and knowledge is more widely distributed, but power remains concentrated. It is shared more than in the left-hand column, but it is not widely distributed, so behaviour remains largely participative. More activity-level talk is required here, but it is confined to a small group who share the power.

Right-hand column ('Value Difference')

This is the domain of the third, *Ic* (integrating) type of learning and AT's 'activity'. The objective is to develop a shared 'big picture', and since this requires an understanding of all the attitudes and views of those involved, difference is meat and drink to both integrative learning and activity. 'The book' is thrown out the window, and attention focuses on relationships between people and their different perceptions.

When power and knowledge are both widely distributed, there is no place for participative action. Most talk has to be at the activity level, and most action has to be collaborative. (Talk of this kind can be quite difficult for those used to working within hierarchies where power is concentrated at the top.)

Strictly speaking, AT's 'activity' occurs in all six boxes of the grid, and all three types of learning, but activity-level conversations have to be more frequent and less exclusive, as one moves from left to right and power and knowledge become more widely distributed. Activity talk can be hardly visible on the left of the grid (it could just be leaders talking to themselves) where operation is the dominant activity, but on the right of the grid it shows up clearly in the much greater efforts people have to make to reveal the hidden agendas and tacit assumptions of their collaborators.

The appropriate level of action or conversation is determined by the context. If you have the power, you can oblige people to participate in the achievement of your objectives; but if you lack the power, you are obliged to 'collaborate'. Equally, where you seek activity-level outcomes, do not be lulled into thinking that operating within the confines of the left-hand column is sufficient. In order to be effective, you need to be able to operate successfully in the new world of the right-hand column, with its quite different demands on those who enter it.

Ways of seeing and knowing: interdisciplinary adventures

The two areas of thinking that have probably contributed most in recent years to the development of a new understanding of business organizations are individual psychology and systems theory. The new mental model that has emerged as a result of the conjunction of these fields exerts a powerful influence on how we see organizations and what (we think) we know about what they are and how they learn and act.

Each has significantly widened our general understanding and at the same time raised further questions, highlighted below, which we will try to answer in subsequent chapters.

Individual psychology

Much of what now seems like 'common sense' in the cultivation of 'learning organizations' comes from ideas, principles and insights developed and tested over the years by students of individual psychology. From this point of view, any theory of organizational behaviour and learning worth its salt must be solidly based on what we know about individual behaviour and learning, because organizations are collections of individuals.

Most learning theories agree that individuals learn when they become aware of inconsistencies with currently held beliefs. Individual learning is the resolution of these contradictions, so organizational learning can thus be seen as the result of a collective awareness of incongruities (such as the need for permanence and change), and their subsequent resolution.

Many have taken this approach further by proposing a parallel between individual life crises and changes in organizations. They suggest that failures to learn are often due to the defensive stratagems (rationalization, denial, etc.) used to protect the organization's stability and sense of identity. Argyris and Schon (1978) say that the organizational learning which is the prerequisite of organizational change is linked to an ability to breach organizational defences by confronting what they call 'espoused theories' (the theories that people give for their behaviour) with 'theories in use' (the theories indicated by their behaviour).

This anthropocentric approach to organizational learning sees individual agency as the main driving force. By invoking the notion of self-managed learning and development, it leads to the idea of the self-developing organization, which fits well with the popular conception of the 'learning organization' as one that continuously transforms itself through the learning it nurtures among its members.

The basic prescriptive premise of this view of organizational learning is that in most organizations the human potential to learn is a vast, largely latent resource which managers must endeavour to tap. But there are some problems with this approach.

It requires the integration of the individual into the whole, but offers no mechanism for achieving this integration, other than the agency of the individuals themselves. Without such a mechanism, the only defence against fragmentation is the sort of unifying vision that 'aligns' (subordinates) the multiple agendas of individuals with (to) that of the leadership. This thinking leads to the dilemma of unity and diversity, and to questions individual psychology cannot answer, like: 'How can we value learn from different perspectives, while retaining a clear sense of direction?'

Systems theory

Systems theory, which has also evolved quite independently of management theory, offers a solution to the paradox of unity and diversity by seeing both organizations and individuals as adaptive systems which modify their behaviour in response to feedback. According to this view (Bateson, 1972), individuals, and thus organizations, are self-regulating organisms which maintain basic stability through a process of error detection and correction that is equivalent to learning.

But as we have seen, there are other kinds of learning which may be much more important in turbulent environments, such as 'integrative' (see above), 'deutero' (learning to learn), and 'double-loop' learning (Argyris and Schon, 1978).

Single-loop learning is simple error detection and correction within the context of a set of unquestioned assumptions. It acts as the system's stabilizing mechanism. It is absolutely necessary for individuals and organizations alike, but it is, by definition, incapable of bringing about change. For this, double-loop learning – learning that questions and is willing to discard some of the assumptions that constrain single-loop learning – is said to be needed. This approach to organizational learning has been popularized by Peter Senge (1990), whose ideas have become the foundations of many 'learning organization' strategies.

An explanation for the great influence Senge's application of systems theory has had on managers is that it resonates well with their experience and the problems they face. The systems approach suggests that as enterprises become more complex, we need more sophisticated models of cause and effect, and must therefore gather and analyse more data. However, this approach becomes ineffective when the system extends beyond corporate boundaries, or when the whole system is 'unknowable' by one individual or group, because in this kind of context one must question whether management can ever understand the whole system and make correct decisions.

Peter Checkland (1981) has argued that the world view of each member of a system is part of the system, and this two-way feedback loop between individual and system means the whole system is unknowable. He developed his Soft Systems Methodology to take account of this intrinsic lack of knowability.

Individual psychology and systems theories have proved rich seams for management writers and thinkers in recent years, and they have been assiduously mined. But it is fair to say that most of the many prescriptions and insights that have emerged from these interdisciplinary adventures have been based on the assumption that although perceptions of reality may vary, there is one unique reality. This leads to the proposal that the role of the leader is to divine the unique reality, and to derive from it a uniquely valid strategy.

This is where we part company from the conventional wisdom: we believe that though enriched by its forays into psychology and the theory of systems, the conventional management wisdom remains locked in an outmoded modernist theory of knowledge that prevents it from grappling effectively with areas of the modern world that are inherently indeterminate.

We are not saying that the management discourse must renounce its faith in analysis or reason. We are saying that it should acknowledge the limits of linear logic, and recognize that the modern world, including management, is becoming infested with problems that cannot be resolved by unique truths.

This historic step from modernism to postmodernism is not an intellectual game. It has already occurred in areas such as mathematics (with Gödel's Incompleteness Theorem) and physics (with Heisenberg's Uncertainty Principle) that once seemed to be the temples of pure reason. Science itself acknowledges the limits of rationality, and other areas, such as linguistics and critical theory, have taken their cue from science and abandoned their assumptions of determinacy, and their faith in uniquely valid answers and solutions.

The postmodernist approach accepts that knowledge and meaning emerge from the way we do things together, in local contexts, rather than from pre-existing, universal structures or truths, as Plato supposed. Just as the position and speed of an electron depends on the point of view of the observer, so our perceptions of 'social' phenomena are influenced by our points of view. We cannot help seeing things in the context of local theories. We cannot look at the world in an objective way, independent of the contexts which give things their local meaning. This is not a failure of our vision; it is a reflection of reality. There is wisdom in the old joke: 'Don't adjust your mind, it's reality that's at fault.'

Different sorts of knowledge enable us to do different sorts of things. The scientific method helps us to do science, for example, but it does not help us manage complex relationships in our increasingly complex business world. Management needs to become postmodernist too, because there are limits to the amount of sense such notions as 'progress', 'rationality' and 'scientific determinacy' can make of our daily lives. (For those interested in the difference between the modernist and postmodernist perspectives, Appendix B poses a number of topical management questions, and compares the sort of answers a modernist perspective would give with the sort of answers one might expect from a postmodernist perspective.)

To work successfully in complex relationships where power is distributed, objectives are provisional and reality is in the eyes of all beholders, managers must abandon the conventional model which sees everything in black and white and as right or wrong, and replace it with an open, multi-coloured model, where logic is fuzzy, conclusions are equivocal and no one is or can be in control. Individual psychology and systems theory have already carried management thinking some distance along this road, but many managers are still struggling to fit their new insights into the old idea that social systems (including partnerships) are knowable and controllable, and are still wondering why reality never quite matches up to their visions.

They need to take one more step, and see relationships, rather than objectives, as the focus of management. They must learn to stop instructing and judging, and devote their efforts to discovering what the members of their organizations perceive, and what they want to do.

The Partnering Grid helps people to take this vital step from the modernist outlook, which says 'The truth is out there,' to the postmodernist outlook, which says 'Difference is out there, and you must learn to live with it.'

In Chapter 4 we will investigate what might be called the 'psychodynamics' of taking these crucial, eastward steps across the grid that are equivalent to leaving conventional wisdoms not behind, but in their place, and embracing a new perspective, more suited to a connected, collective world.

After that, we will devote the rest of this book to using the Partnering Grid and the 'tools for thought' embedded in it as a map to help us explore the strange new management world on the far right of the grid.

Summary

The conventional, modernist approach to management cannot deal with the complexity and ambiguity of partnership enterprise.

The Partnering Grid incorporates tools for thought that are more appropriate for the new era.

These tools re-frame critical management problems and their solutions by questioning the basic assumptions involved.

The Partnering Grid is a postmodernist tool that helps managers to shift their focus from objectives to relationships.

References

Argyris, C. and Schon, D. (1978) *Organizational Learning: A Theory in Action Perspective*, Addison-Wesley.

Bateson, G. (1972) *Steps to an Ecology of Mind*, Intertext.

Checkland, P. (1981) *Systems Thinking, Systems Practice*, John Wiley.

Pedler, M., Burgoyne, J. and Boydell, T. (1991) *The Learning Company: A Strategy for Sustainable Development*, McGraw-Hill.

Senge, P. (1990) *The Fifth Discipline*, Doubleday.

4   Searching for 'fit'

The Partnering Grid described in Chapter 2 identifies six basic perceptions of partnership defined by 'Ambition' on the vertical axis and 'View of Difference' on the horizontal axis, which can be used to analyse individual and collective perceptions of any partnership.

Perceptions are not facts, of course, but a set of perceptions and the differences between them can shed new and sometimes surprising light on relationships, and help the partners to understand each other better and therefore work together more effectively.

In this chapter we will show how managers can use the grid's mapping to assess how far their perceptions of the partnering relationship, and those of their partners, suit the 'context' of the partnership, and so indicate the likelihood of success. We will explore steps to improve 'fit', and see how the power and knowledge characteristics of the partnering organizations help to determine the most appropriate moves.

By 'context' we mean a combination of three key factors:

- the external environment in which the partnering takes place

- the style of the partnering organizations (their cultures and distributions of power and knowledge)
- the objectives of the partnership (see Figure 4.1).

For example, 'Command and Control' is a perfectly appropriate box for a relationship in which power and knowledge are concentrated, but much less appropriate (and hence less effective) when power and knowledge are widely distributed. Similarly, the 'command and control' approach suits a defensive relationship designed to preserve the status quo, but not an ambitious relationship that seeks synergy and co-creation.

Mistaking the appropriate box is a common cause of partnering failure, and perhaps the most common misjudgement of context is to assume, and to act as if, you have more power than you really do. When partnerships go wrong, it is usually because someone in control has misjudged the context, and adopted an approach or a style that is at odds with how others perceive the distributions of power and knowledge.

It follows from this that the way to establish if the box you perceive yourself to be in is appropriate for the context is to ask your partners what box they think you are in. 'Fit' in partnerships comes from talking and discussing. You are never where you think you are; you are where others perceive you to be.

Improving 'fit'

One of the most striking things to emerge from our partnering research was how anxious all of our research partners were to find 'the answer' to good partnering. Most wanted a standard, general-purpose solution, despite the fact that the research clearly showed that some approaches to partnering were widely seen to be more successful in some contexts than in others.

It is important to resist the very natural temptation to view movement up and to the right of the grid as a developmental process. The appropriateness or otherwise of a box depends on the context, what led each partner to join the partnership in the first place, and what inspires them to remain in it.

Environment	Style	Objectives
Command and Control • Immediate threat • Predictable, knowable environment • Little external regulation • Few significant stakeholders • Widely available resources	• Preference for formality, structure, compliance • Power comes from the top • Knowledge distribution based on bureaucracy and hierarchy	• Response to low-choice situation (e.g. bankruptcy, take-over) • Maintain stability and manage risk (e.g. integration of operations)
Hearts and Minds • Steady incremental growth opportunities • Predictable, knowable environment • Little external regulation • Few significant stakeholders • Widely available resources	• Preference for harmony, shared vision • Unitary, dominant power • Limited knowledge distribution, held in cultures and values	• Optimize existing products/services in existing markets • New products/services in existing markets • Explore new markets with aligned cultures

Arm's Length
• External barriers to operations (e.g. regulatory, cultural)
• Growing unpredictability
• Tight regulation
• Widening stakeholder community
• Strong competition
• Scarce resources
	• Preference for minimal movement
	• Focus on clear communications
	• Sharing of power, control and ownership in order to share risks
	• Knowledge widely distributed, centrally held and orchestrated
		• Minimal partnerings to:
		  – Overcome external barriers
		  – Reduce costs
		  – Share risks

Do and Review
• Turbulent change, significant expansion opportunities
• Growing unpredictability
• Tight regulation
• Widening stakeholder community
• Strong competition
• Scarce resources
	• Preference for collaboration, learning, flexibility
	• Strong process orientation
	• Sharing of power, control and ownership
	• Knowledge widely distributed, attempts at central sense-making
		• Technological/product innovation in new markets
		  – Incremental change
		  – Cyclical improvements
		• Expansion within turbulent markets

Gridlock • Strong constraining external forces (regulatory, market) • Multiple influential stakeholders • Resources threatened	• Preference for control by commitment • Knowledge treated as private: seen to be fragmented and held within power bases • Operation of multiple, conflicting power sources	• Compromise to stabilize political situation • Defence against conflicting purposes • Keeping everyone happy: face-saving paramount
Radically New • Complex, discontinuous change • Low predictability • Broad and influential stakeholder community	• Preference for involvement, challenge and dialogue • Power and ownership accepted as widely spread • Knowledge is treated as public: seen to reside within network of relationships	• Pre-empt change with degree and speed of innovation • Create radically new ways of working and/or product/service offerings • Optimize creativity and transformation

Figure 4.1   Partnering contexts

Environment is part of the context, and the appropriateness of a particular grid location depends partly on environmental qualities such as stability, resource availability, exposure to external control (for example, the degree of regulation), patterns of ownership, the influence and vociferousness of non-owning stakeholders and, above all, on the distribution of power.

The primary dimension on the grid that must 'fit' context is 'View of Difference'. It is 'horses for courses' – there are some contexts in which avoiding difference is fitting, and others where tolerating or valuing difference is more appropriate.

'Hearts and minds' and 'command and control' are suitable approaches if the world is stable and predictable. Those with power know what has to be done, and see their task as ensuring that it is done well.

If the world becomes less predictable and people realize that if the enterprise cannot learn as fast as its environment is changing it may perish, 'do and review' or 'arm's length' approaches become more suitable, and efforts should be made to construct feedback loops, get everyone 'closer to the customer', and use so-called 'boundary workers' to scan the environment and gather intelligence.

Building on the model developed by Tom Boydell of the Learning Company Project (see Figure 2.2) enables us to make general observations about the sorts of styles most appropriate to different contexts.

Difference-minimizing organizations always seek stability, and will often try to use partnerships to 'stabilize' what appear to them to be uncomfortably volatile environments. The partnering styles in 'hearts and minds' and 'command and control' are both transactional, but the objectives differ. The 'hearts and minds' organization enters partnerships to achieve goals it could not have pursued on its own, while the 'command and control' organization tends to see its partnering as a way of managing risk.

Difference-managing organizations always seek adaptability in turbulent and competitive environments. The partnering styles in both 'do and review' and 'arm's length' approaches are process-oriented, but the objectives differ. The 'do and review' organization enters into partnerships to adapt to a new or changed context and pursue goals it could not have pursued on its own, whereas the 'arm's length' organization sees partnering as a way to 'manage' risk by sharing it.

Difference-valuing organizations seek to transform themselves in unpredictable environments through collaborative advantage (different from competitive advantage, in that it works with and does not try to dominate its environment). The partnering styles in 'radically new' and 'gridlock' both focus attention on the relationships themselves, but beliefs differ. 'Radically new' organizations believe that wonderful things could happen, and probably will, whereas 'gridlock' organizations believe wonderful things could happen, but probably won't. People in 'gridlock' help to fulfil their own pessimistic prophesies by refusing, in the interests of maintaining 'stability', to let go of their personal agendas.

Movement in the grid is desirable when it becomes clear that the existing grid location or style is inappropriate for the environment (either because the environment was not properly understood at the outset, or because it has changed), or when the objectives have changed (because they have been achieved, or because partners wish to embark on projects that require a closer, longer-term relationship). More movement is indicated when both environments and objectives change, of course.

However, it is easier to describe the circumstances in which grid movement is desirable than to recognize and respond to them. For one thing, it is often hard to know when the environment has changed and different objectives are more appropriate, and for another, most organizations lack the chameleon's ability to adapt instantly to new environments. They become wedded to and comfortable with a particular partnering style, and even when the weaknesses of 'command and control', for example, in a partnership where power and knowledge are widely distributed, become obvious to all but the most dyed-in-the-wool commander and controller, it can be hard to come to terms with the need to replace the organization's central 'brain' with a new kind of system that can rapidly distil a collective interpretation from many views.

An important dynamic in partnering, therefore, is the tension between the partner's perception of the environment and its preferred style. This does not mean that styles should always be sacrificed on the altar of context, because the partners' preferred styles or grid locations are important parts of the context, but it does mean that grid location should never be taken for granted.

Take the case of an organization that decides the only way to counter its competitors is to form a partnership with another firm to develop new leading-edge products. Its environment is risky and highly regulated, and so more suited to a project-based 'do and review' style. However, its partner prides itself on having a 'radically new' style, well suited to innovation. The organization has a number of options. It can:

- test the validity of its view of the partnering environment by asking other interested parties for their perceptions
- review the partnership's objectives in the light of any new information that emerges, and modify them if necessary
- try to adapt its partnering style more fully to the context.

If the testing validates the organization's initial view, and if the value of the prospective additional revenues and the potential fortification of its market position are considered too valuable to relinquish, the organization has no option but to take its fate in its hands and attempt to navigate the virtual waters of the grid.

Navigating the grid

A word of warning for grid navigators: our research suggests that the bottom left and bottom right boxes are both powerful attractors in the 'Partnering Style' space.

Static, unmanaged relationships tend to slip down to the left because of the standard practice of leaving partnership management to the conventional gatekeepers of our processes, such as accountants and lawyers, whose professions predispose them to a 'command and control' style.

We have also found a strong pull towards the bottom right. As wider distributions of power, knowledge and purpose transform our environment, more and more partnerships find that no one party has control over enough of the agenda to navigate a straight course. As each of the constituencies defend their patch and try to control the outcomes, the partnership slips deeper and deeper into 'gridlock'.

This is both bad news and good news: bad because to remain in 'gridlock' for long can often be fatal for the partnership, as partners move elsewhere ('command and control' at least has the merit of being able to insist on action); good because, apart from the crucial ability to let go of the illusion of control, all the elements of a creative, 'radically new' partnership are in place.

If an organization needs to improve its 'fit' for any of the reasons outlined above, and wishes to avoid being trapped by the 'command and control' and 'gridlock' attractors, it needs to understand the dynamics influencing its position and those of its partners.

Once a partnership perception has been located on the grid by the sort of exercise described in Appendix A, there are three general directions in which perceptions can move:

- vertically (along the 'Ambition' axis)
- horizontally (along the 'View of Difference' axis)
- and diagonally (along both axes at the same time).

However, it is important to recognize that the initial positions (of individual partners and the partnership itself) are never absolute. The grid plots perceptions, and there are all sorts of different ways in which partnerships can be and are seen, both by partners themselves and by outsiders. When we say a partner or a partnership is in a certain box, we are saying that from the point of view of this person or group, this is where the partner or partnership seems to be.

But the subjective nature of a grid position does not prevent 'movement' within the grid. All it says is that the direction and extent of movement will also be subjective, and will thus be perceived differently by different people. Movement on the grid is a mental not a physical event. It occurs as a result of conversations, and is apparent in changes in behaviour and the way people talk about the relationship and act within it.

It is also important to recognize that movement in the grid is rarely the result of deliberate intent. It is much more often the consequence of forgetting and keeping private (down and to the left) or becoming aware of and making public (up and to the right) one's own assumptions. In other words, movement occurs when the veil of ignorance about the motivations and beliefs of those involved in the partnership is lifted or lowered.

Moving diagonally

Diagonal movement is challenging, because it involves changes in both dimensions – ambition and view of difference.

To put the point another way, partners in diagonally adjacent boxes perceive different realities, and will find it very hard to form productive relationships without major adjustments to their general outlooks.

This does not mean that diagonal partnering should or can be avoided, however. All enterprises (integrated organizations as well as partnerships) include people whose perceptions of their relationships with internal or external partners are in diagonal relationships with one another on the grid. Whether or not a change in perceptions is appropriate depends not on how hard it is to change, but on how far existing perceptions are from perceptions that fit the context.

Moreover, the geometry of the grid suggests that diagonal movement is just a short cut to a new position which can be reached by one vertical and one horizontal move. The challenge is to cut loose from existing perceptions and head in a north-easterly direction, despite the siren calls of the attractors at the bottom left and bottom right of the grid. In other words, once in motion, perceptions need to be actively steered not merely towards the desired positions, but also away from the default positions.

In order to build a clearer picture of the composite diagonal shift, we need to explore the dynamic natures of vertical and horizontal movement more closely.

Moving vertically

Vertical movement is easier than diagonal movement, and by the same token, partners occupying boxes directly above or below each other are usually more 'compatible' and can form stable relationships more readily. But because the quality that drives vertical movement up the grid is trust, and trust is easy to lose, it is movement that can quickly be reversed.

Partners who are intolerant of differences but ambitious for the partnership, for instance, may decide 'command and control' is too constraining, and try to move to 'hearts and minds'. If trust fails to develop or if either partner feels that their trust is betrayed or not fully reciprocated, the relationship is likely to end or revert to 'command and control' operated by the dominant partner. (The characteristic features of 'command and control' can also be perpetuated or even imposed by those who are commanded and controlled, when they resist change.)

According to a recent study by Bleeke and Ernst (1995), 80% of joint ventures end in a sale by one partner to the other. In the language of the grid, this suggests a strong tendency for power to become more concentrated as a partnership develops, and for the style of those in power to default to 'command and control'. This is natural: 'command and control' is appropriate when power is concentrated in the hands of one partner, as it tends to become when a partnership runs into difficulties.

As we have already noted, there is a time element in vertical movement, in the sense that ambitious partnerships tend to be perceived as long-term. It is this perceived durability that makes it worth spending the time and effort it often takes to cultivate trust, which – in principle, at any rate – is a more efficient way to ensure reciprocity in a partnership than a tightly worded contract, diligently policed.

On being asked which leg it moved first, the centipede became rooted to the spot. Trust is like that: the more one focuses on it, the more elusive it becomes. Trust and the lack of it are not the causes of success and failure in partnering; they are merely symptoms. They emerge from the way people speak to each other, and the only way to foster the emergence of trust is to find new ways of talking.

Those who have used the Partnering Grid have said it provides a way to discuss what turn out to be the foundations of trust without talking about trust itself. They have discovered that it is often better to contrast differing grid positions and explore their origins than to endeavour deliberately to build trust.

A focus on the lack of trust itself often fuels a culture of blame and suspicion that makes things worse. Trust comes from action. We need to switch the spotlight from the relationship to the task, search for actions we can agree that we need to take, and allow trust to emerge spontaneously from working together successfully.

The secret of building trust, for an individual, is to become more trustworthy oneself by being honest about one's motives. The 'conscience' of each partner can be strengthened through joint teams charged with recording the partnership's learning history, for example. Outsiders can be helpful here, because they are far less inclined to rewrite history. Receptiveness to the messages they generate is crucial, but hard to achieve without coaching and feedback.

Disjunctures in the vertical dimension may reflect differences in how the risks of the partnership are perceived. Reaching a common understanding of how risks and opportunities are seen by each partner, and establishing mechanisms for updating it, can help to add upward momentum to perceptions. Standard risk assessment tools that allow parties to state their opinions of quantitative and qualitative risk can also enhance mutual understanding, but more credence should be given to intuition than numbers, because 'gut feel' has more impact on behaviour and perceptions.

It is all too easy for partners to get locked into discussion habits that make vertical movement difficult to initiate and maintain. If every proposal is greeted with a chorus of 'Yes, but ...', the most optimistic of partners will find it hard to maintain their initial enthusiasm. Careful use of techniques such as Edward De Bono's 'thinking hats' (De Bono, 1985), which insist on the recognition of opportunity before the statement of risk, can help sustain upward momentum.

Moving horizontally

Although horizontal movement is in many ways more challenging than vertical movement, there is frequently more to be gained from it, for at least two reasons: first, because moving from a policy of minimizing difference to a policy of tolerating it expands the choice of partners; and second, because tolerance of difference makes relationships intrinsically more robust.

Indeed, it is our belief that moving perceptions horizontally across the 'View of Difference' dimension, in pursuit of better fit with context, is much the most effective way to increase the performance of partnerships where power and knowledge are widely distributed. In other words: if you want to change, change the way you see difference.

The difficulty with this kind of movement is that people tend to cling more fiercely to their approaches to difference than to their partnership ambitions. Everyone is for trust, just as everyone is against sin. The merits of associating oneself with an alien culture, and thereby running a risk of cultural infection, are far less compelling. By and large, 'command and control' and 'hearts and minds' cultures will be very reluctant to move to 'arm's length' and 'do and review' relationships while other options remain available.

The reason for the general reluctance to move to the right of the grid is that such movement requires people to abandon a number of basic assumptions about how their systems operate, and change their 'theories in use' (as opposed to 'espoused theories') about difference. People may say they tolerate or value difference, but behave in ways that indicate a wish to minimize it. 'Theories in use' must change if movement to the right of the grid is to be achieved.

The so-called 'globalization' of business is putting pressure on organizations to bite the bullet of easterly movement, for the simple reason that a refusal to move to the right becomes a self-imposed strategic straitjacket. No organization can be truly global while it refuses to enter into partnerships with organizations that have developed within different cultures.

Figure 4.2 shows how the shifts from 'minimizing' to 'managing' and then to 'exploiting' difference challenge various assumptions about how enterprises are organized, and highlight the implications of an intent to move in the horizontal plane.

One virtue of this diagram is that it can reveal discrepancies between Argyris's espoused theories, and theories in use. When people acknowledge that power is distributed but continue to treat systems as 'given', insist on denying uncertainty and resolving differences, impose their organization's 'persona' or sense of self from the top or learn only from their own experiences, it is reasonable to assume they are being either unrealistic or disingenuous, and have a long way to go before they can achieve genuine horizontal movement.

It is worth emphasizing again, however, that movement from the left to the right of the grid is not a natural developmental path. Movement can be in any open direction, and the merits or otherwise of particular boxes depend on context. The ultimate test of the suitability of a box is whether or not it works. If

	Minimize Difference	Manage Difference	Exploit Difference
Power (ways of working)	Centralized, concentrated	'Shared' – teams, empowerment	Distributed, devolved, disaggregated
Change	Systems imposed or given	Systems can be improved	Systems emerge – worked by everyone
Uncertainty	None	Coping, adaptation	Inevitable – collective enquiry
Understanding of Partner	Through problem-resolution	By working together	Through hearing differences
Knowing one's own Organization	From the top	At the interface with the partner	From everyone's perspective
Learning	Memory, best practice	Adaptation	Mutuality, dialogue
	Avoid	Tolerate	Value

Figure 4.2   Revealing assumptions

'Command and Control' works, do not try to fix it. Moving in the grid requires profound changes in the partners' attitudes to power, knowledge and learning, and as weather experts say after a snowstorm: 'Don't travel unless it is absolutely necessary.'

Shifting patterns of power

Figure 4.3 shows that when power is concentrated in the hands of individuals or groups who claim the right to define the enterprise and identify its problems and solutions, difference is seen as something to be avoided or minimized with common standards and compelling visions, and other members of the enterprise are only consulted to ensure compliance and 'buy-in' (see Chapter 5).

Nowadays, moving from the minimization to the toleration of difference is often inspired by a recognition of the need for empowerment and decentralization to permit local flexibility

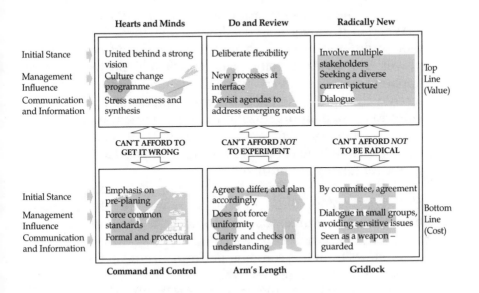

	Hearts and Minds	Do and Review	Radically New	
Initial Stance Management Influence Communication and Information	United behind a strong vision Culture change programme Stress sameness and synthesis	Deliberate flexibility New processes at interface Revisit agendas to address emerging needs	Involve multiple stakeholders Seeking a diverse current picture Dialogue	Top Line (Value)
	CAN'T AFFORD TO GET IT WRONG	CAN'T AFFORD *NOT* TO EXPERIMENT	CAN'T AFFORD *NOT* TO BE RADICAL	
Initial Stance Management Influence Communication and Information	Emphasis on pre-planing Force common standards Formal and procedural	Agree to differ, and plan accordingly Does not force uniformity Clarity and checks on understanding	By committee, agreement Dialogue in small groups, avoiding sensitive issues Seen as a weapon – guarded	Bottom Line (Cost)
	Command and Control	Arm's Length	Gridlock	

Figure 4.3 Revealing management processes

and accommodate local needs. But the grid reveals that power and its distribution are far from simple.

Kinds of power

There is a growing acceptance nowadays that power should be distributed more widely than in the past, in the interests of the organization's speed of response and general agility, but the tacit belief remains that power is homogeneous and can be shifted around an organization more or less at will.

When managers speak of 'empowerment', for instance, they mean a process of taking power from one stratum of an organization (usually middle management, and usually achieved by sacking middle managers) and giving it to other strata (operatives or 'customer-facing' staff, for example).

But organizational power is clearly not homogeneous. The kind of power engineers trade in, for instance, is quite different from the kind of power possessed by a financial controller or human resources (HR) manager. HR people will deny vehemently that they are about power at all, and will say their stock in trade is meaning and caring, but this too is power.

Whether it is over material, knowledge, ideology, strategy or money, different people are always trading in different kinds of power. The heterogeneity of organizational power is seldom apparent, because its various manifestations are exercised in different ways and spoken of in different languages, but those who want to change an organization's power structure need to recognize its heterogeneity and complexity. They need to make all these different kinds of power apparent and find a common language for talking about them.

One way to approach the problem is to recognize that although there are different kinds of power, all ultimately issue from the same source: their contribution to the performance of the enterprise, whether it be a company or a partnership.

It follows from this common performance-related provenance of power that one reason why different people or functions speak of power in different languages is that the measurability of their contributions to performance vary. For instance, if the contributions of HR managers to enterprise performance could be measured as precisely as the contributions of engineers or treasury managers, their languages might converge.

There is much to be said, therefore, for making great efforts to clarify and make less equivocal the contributions of all the various players or partners to the overall performance of the enterprise. This is not the place to attempt to construct a common language of performance, but we accept that it will be hard, for at least two reasons: first, some performance is naturally hard to measure; second, other activities, although measurable, affect performance in indirect ways. One can see a footballer expending a lot of energy, for example, running up the pitch, a long way from the ball. He seems to be making no obvious contribution to the play those close to the ball are developing, but he may draw defenders away and make more space for his teammates as they approach the goal.

The reason that such subtle collaborative strategies are much more common within areas of expertise or specialization than between them is that they depend for their development on a common language. Partners cannot see all of the ways they can collaborate while their 'hinterlands' (the competences, dreams and networks they bring with them) remain obscured from each other by professional jargon and the linguistic nuances of their corporate and professional cultures.

With the help of transcendent languages such as the grid, all the various languages of power can be induced to converge by changing the currencies they deal in.

Times of power

Another reason why managers find it hard to change the 'power structures' of their organizations is their assumption that once people acquire power, they should keep it. People can be stripped of power if they fail to make good use of it, but as long as they prove themselves worthy of power, it is generally assumed they have a right to it.

As we move to the right, however, the nature and use of power changes. People must tolerate or value difference when power is widely distributed. When power cannot be possessed by or embodied in an individual or group, it becomes just a mobile source of co-ordinating energy that can only be bor-rowed for a while, and only with the consent of others.

In 'Radically New' – the most appropriate box if both power and knowledge are widely distributed – people can only hold power on behalf of others, and only if their partners agree that it is in everyone's interests for them to do so. That may sound a bit pious, but it is no more than an acknowledgement of the logic of the context. How else can a partnership operate when power and knowledge are widely distributed?

The philosophies on the right of the grid emerge in response to the wider distributions of power and knowledge. People are moti-vated to behave differently not by some noble desire for equality or democracy, but because they want the partnership to perform.

Our discussion of Activity Theory in Chapter 3 suggested that power not only moves from person to person and group to group; its pattern of distribution also changes from time to time, in accordance with changes in the nature of the task at hand.

Bob Lewis (see page 57) has noted how patterns of power shift during successive stages of a research project. When the team undertaking the research project first assembles, it needs as 'democratic' a structure as possible, because although it has an overall objective and a shared language, it has no plan.

Once a list of tasks has been democratically agreed, the most efficient next step is for the team to split into sub-teams expert in specific task areas, on the understanding that the whole team will re-convene once these initial tasks have been completed. When the main team divides its labour in this way, a new power structure becomes appropriate. Each sub-team can operate dem-ocratically, but the need emerges for some kind of co-ordinator. While the main team is split into a set of sub-teams, someone must be ceded the power he or she needs to act as an orchestra-tor or gatekeeper of the methodology.

This switch from democracy to a more monarchical distribu-tion of power occurs in various ways, depending on the history of existing relationships. In some cases there is a 'prince in wait-ing' whom everyone accepts. In other cases, a prince may be 'elected' during the initial democratic stage of the project. Someone may say something that seems to capture the spirit of the meeting, and be 'rewarded' with the role of 'co-ordinator' for the next stage of the project.

The scientific research team (of which more in our discussion of leadership in Chapter 8) is a good example of a collective enterprise where power and knowledge are distributed to some extent. It requires 'conventional' leaders from time to time, to whom power is surrendered temporarily, on condition that it is exercised appropriately.

This is the kind of situation where the partnering approaches of the middle of the grid ('arm's length' and 'do and review') are appropriate – step-by-step approaches, within the constraints of rules and conventions. When difference is ineradicable, it has to be tolerated; and toleration requires and is revealed by styles of behaviour and talk that are quite distinct from those of 'hearts and minds' and 'command and control'.

When power and knowledge are widely distributed, there can be no recourse to this part-time leadership model, because there are not enough rules and conventions that everyone will agree to. Difference is ignored in the left-hand column and managed in the middle column, but in the right-hand column it is celebrated as the prime mover of the partnership. From being a problem to be solved or a fact of life to be lived with, it becomes life itself, and moreover, life that can easily be dimmed or extinguished if people start throwing their weight around.

It is helpful here to build on Activity Theory and take it one step further in the context of the grid. AT's distinction between 'operations', 'actions' and 'activity' is a useful framework for thinking about how people interact, but it contains the clear implication that someone or some group has the power to decide when a change of 'level' is needed.

In contexts where 'radically new' is appropriate, everyone must be free to question everything, at any time, and space should always be available for activity-level conversations and the collective interpretation they generate. When constant change is a quality of everything, from the business environment to the personal hinterlands of collaborators, it is not enough to convene an occasional activity-level meeting where normal rules are suspended. Normal rules have to be retired, period.

As we will see in Chapter 7, this does not mean that 'radically new' partnerships are always and inevitably 'out of control'. They cannot be controlled, but they can be 'in control', by virtue of the common ground and the common wish to explore it. Power in the 'radically new' approach becomes detached from people and groups, and acquires a roving commission.

Summary

The concept of power we have described sees it as a source of co-ordinating energy that moves around and assumes different patterns of distribution according to context. On the left of the grid it is concentrated, in the middle of the grid it is shared, and on the right of the grid it belongs to no one, but is available to anyone.

It is a hard concept to implement in integrated organizations because the old concept of power as embodied and static is so robust. It is hard, for example, to be open and candid about your opinions and plans with those in whose hands your career lies. We tend to defer rather than contradict in situations where our careers and life-plans could be put in jeopardy by an unguarded remark or an unwisely brutal frankness.

In ambitious partnerships that value difference, however, the perception of power as mobile and fluid is essential, because static power structures obscure the differences of which the partnership's opportunity set consists, and effectively outlaw the instabilities on which its energy and creativity both depend. (See Chapter 6 for a discussion of the implications for strategy of intrinsically unpredictable environments.)

But to learn to live with and use this concept of power, the enterprise needs to open a space where people can understand each other and appreciate the full richness and complexity of their relationships.

Similar considerations apply to assumptions about structures and systems. Whereas the difference-minimization strategy takes structures and systems as given, the difference-toleration strategy sees both as improvable, through learning loops and feedback. The language of transactions is thus replaced by the language of improvement; of Total Quality Management and

Business Process Re-engineering; of doing things better and faster and becoming fitter and leaner.

This reflects shifts across the Pedler, Burgoyne and Boydell classification of types of organizational learning, described in Chapter 3 (see page 53). Moving from the minimization to the toleration of difference requires a shift in emphasis from implementing to improving; and moving from tolerating to valuing difference requires a similar shift in emphasis from improving to integrating.

All three learning types occur in almost every enterprise, of course, but movement to the right requires learning to become 'richer' in the learning type characteristic of each attitude to difference. You cannot be said to be genuinely tolerant of difference, for example, if you are not doing a lot more of the 'improving' type of learning than is common in 'command and control' or 'hearts and minds'.

To summarize: movement in the grid, which is mental rather than physical, can take the form of an unintentional slippage or an intentional step to improve 'fit'. Movement can often be started by plotting the existing positions of partners on the grid, because simply talking about difference in the language of the grid can cause some degree of horizontal movement (see page 79).

Many of those who have used the grid say it was particularly helpful when struggling with 'relationship' issues. However, some say that although it was relatively easy to locate their own styles on the grid, it was harder to locate the styles of their partners, because without true dialogue (of which more later) it was easy to mistake a 'command and control' partner, for example, for a 'hearts and minds' or 'do and review' partner.

Understanding one's partners is often hard, because it may be in their interests to masquerade as something other than they are. Even when no deception is intended, the style displayed at the beginning of a relationship may be unrepresentative of the partner's true style, in the same way that companies that put all their efforts into selling make promises about after-sales service they are not equipped to keep.

We will therefore devote the rest of this chapter to a rough-and-ready guide to partnering styles, beginning with a brief summary of the 'Views of Difference' characteristic of each of the three columns of the grid.

Understanding each other

In 'hearts and minds' and 'command and control', the conceptions partner organizations have of themselves are provided by the 'leadership', who have little interest in how their organizations are perceived by their partners.

When partners are also required to do as they are told, there is no need to understand them. Difference is ignored because, as far as the partnership is concerned, it does not exist. If difference emerges, it is seen as recalcitrance. According to this view, a proper 'understanding' between partners is only achieved when difference has been eradicated.

In 'arm's length' and 'do and review', it is accepted that people and partners are different, and that the only way for them to understand each other and to learn to work together, despite their differences, is to involve everyone in the processes of partnership; hence the formation of inter-company and inter-disciplinary teams to undertake joint process re-engineering projects, for example.

Elaborate systems are often developed in this central area of the grid to manage interfaces between the processes of each partner and to monitor the quality of understanding, so that although partners speak in different languages, they achieve meetings of minds. The measure of understanding is the extent to which misunderstandings are eliminated.

When there is 360-degree feedback at partnership interfaces, people are very interested in how their partners see them, and make great efforts to discourage the use of stereotypes (including those generated by the grid!) and to foster an understanding of themselves and each other.

When contemplating a move on the grid, the important thing to remember is that although environment and objectives are key considerations when deciding what kind of style to adopt, the fact that both can change means that the relationship itself has a significance that transcends context. It has a special claim on the partners, because if its interests are ignored there may be no partnership to adapt to the new context or to pursue the new objective.

Bearing this thought in mind, let us now see what clues about where on the grid people are located can be gleaned from their general attitudes and behaviour.

Seeing others from 'hearts and minds'

Partners in 'hearts and minds' will have reason to believe they are dealing with partners in:

- 'command and control', if they insist on doing everything by 'the book', and on everything being in 'the book'; if they do not appear to trust you, and 'build the divorce into the marriage ceremony'; if they exercise power through written agreements and the threat of divorce, and if you feel suffocated by their rules and regulations, and frustrated by their defensiveness and their slow-moving processes
- 'arm's length', if they seem wary of your visions and missions; say 'yes' to your way, but carry on doing things their way; seem distant and secretive about their values and purposes, and they exercise power by refusing to return your calls, and insisting on doing things differently, to prove a point
- 'do and review', if there is a new agenda at each meeting, and their need to meet and design new processes seems insatiable; if they always seem to be starting their next change project; if they cannot even agree themselves about what should happen next; if they are always asking for more data or results and keep moving the goalposts, and if they exercise power by threatening to leave the partnership when you refuse to tell them something
- 'gridlock', if they seem unmotivated, and lacking in leadership and vision, but refuse to accept your vision; if they veto things just when you are getting enthusiastic, and if they do not try to exercise any power and keep retreating into their shell

- 'radically new', if they lack conventional leadership and seem indecisive and woolly; if it is hard to see what they want; if they make no sense half the time, but push your comfort zones in unexpected ways; if they seem deeply interested (sometimes alarmingly so) in the way you do things, and if they exercise power, if you can call it that, by carrying on regardless.

Seeing others from 'command and control'

Those in 'command and control' will have reason to believe they are dealing with partners in:

- 'hearts and minds', if they are always reluctant to put things in writing; if everything seems to be about values; if they all say much the same thing; if they are always talking about 'creativity' or 'synergy'; if they seem blind to threats, and if they exercise power by quietly excluding you or urging you to accept their vision
- 'arm's length', if they make the simplest of things problematic and are always asking you to 'clarify your position'; if they insist on doing things their own way, and if they make it very clear that they are willing to give so much, and no more
- 'do and review', if their demands for information are downright presumptuous (they are very nosy); if the rules change every time you meet; if their appetite for change is insatiable, and if they are naively trusting, but never seem satisfied
- 'gridlock', if they lack vision, motivation and leadership; if they always have a reason not to act, and if they appear both weak and stubborn
- 'radically new', if their processes seem anarchic; if it is hard to know who is in charge; if they take the participative style to extremes; if decisions take for ever; if discussions about finance and value are particularly difficult, and if you find it hard to get a handle on where they are coming from.

Seeing others from 'arm's length'

People in 'arm's length' will have reason to believe they are dealing with partners in:

- 'hearts and minds', if they are a little too pally and you feel suffocated, and if you get the feeling they do not approve of the way you do things, but avoid confrontation
- 'command and control', if they are resistant to change; if your suggestions for improvements go unheeded; if you see more or less eye to eye on risk management; if they insist on a plan; if nothing happens unless you get the approval of the 'right person', and if you become frustrated by their inflexibility
- 'do and review', if they ask for too much information; if their continuous improvement initiatives work well; if they seem to be dissatisfied with your lack of creativity, and if you find it hard to trust them completely
- 'gridlock', if their morale seems low and they have no sense of direction; if they obstruct more often than they construct, and if they suddenly lose interest, for no apparent reason
- 'radically new', if their processes seem anarchic and they have no interest in 'best practices' or financial matters; if you can never be sure you are talking to the right person, and if they always want to discuss things with their colleagues, but act quickly and decisively as soon as agreement is reached.

Seeing others from 'do and review'

People in 'do and review' will have reason to believe they are dealing with partners in:

- 'hearts and minds', if they clearly dislike your 'continuous improvement' programmes; if they insist on doing things their way; if they seem very people-oriented; if they care more for values than processes, and if you like the way they are always looking for the creative solution
- 'command and control', if it is very hard to talk to them about improvement; if they seem secretive; if they get annoyed when proper procedures are not followed; if they keep referring to 'the contract'; if they lack creativity, and if the person who makes the decisions is always too busy
- 'arm's length', if you make good progress with processes at the interface; if they always keep their distance; if they appear defensive, and if they emphasize their differences

- 'gridlock', if their eyes glaze over if you start to talk about how partnership processes could be improved; if they seem to lack motivation and leadership, and if they seem blind to the opportunities
- 'radically new', if it seems like an exciting place to work; if there is a lot of creativity, and if they listen to you.

Seeing others from 'gridlock'

People in 'gridlock' will have reason to believe they are dealing with partners in:

- 'hearts and minds', if they appear intolerant of difference; if they seem too wedded to their 'vision'; if their power system is very centralized, and if, despite their protestations about the need for participation, they are unwilling to share power and always claim to have the 'right' answer
- 'command and control', if they seem far too formal; if they are unable to adapt to changed circumstances; if they keep going on about 'the contract', and if they are sticklers for detailed plans and the 'right way'
- 'arm's length', if they do not appear to trust you; if they play their cards close to their chests, and if they do not seem to be interested in your ideas
- 'do and review', if they usually see things your way; if they are easy to get along with; if their focus is on incremental change, and if you feel they should trust you a little more than they seem to
- 'radically new', if you begin to suspect you are your own worst enemy and it is your defensiveness and lack of trust that is the problem.

When dealing with those in the left and middle columns of the grid, people in 'gridlock' tend to feel powerless, frustrated and misunderstood, but may suspect that, in their efforts to be understood, they are limiting the partnership's potential.

Seeing others when aiming at 'radically new'

People who wish to move to 'radically new' will have reason to believe they are dealing with partners in:

- 'hearts and minds', if they cannot tolerate difference; if they seem too wedded to shared visions; if they have a centralized power system, and if they talk a lot about collaboration but keep insisting that their way is best
- 'command and control', if they seem far too formal; if they are unable to adapt to changing circumstances, and if they insist the only way to get things done is to follow tried and tested procedures and abide by the letter of the contract
- 'arm's length', if they do not seem to trust you enough; if they play their cards close to their chests, and if they do not seem very open to new ideas
- 'do and review', if they generally see things your way; if they are easy to get along with; if their focus is on 'incremental change', and if you feel their people need to trust you more
- 'gridlock', if they seem unadventurous; if they are attracted to your culture, and if they find their culture frustrating and dispiriting but are reluctant to change it.

But if the organization's attempt to move to 'radically new' is successful, its members will soon become aware that all their perceptions are prejudices, and will try to put them to one side.

They will resist any temptation to persuade their partners to change, because they will know that no perception of what the partnership is or should be is uniquely valid. They will see the grid as a set of positions, all of which can be occupied by anyone, or any organization, at any time, depending on the context in which they find themselves.

Instead of trying to exhort, seduce and cajole their partners into different attitudes, or different positions on the grid, they will accept other positions as valid and look for common ground to act on, despite the differences.

'Radically new' is a strange place – entering it is rather like entering a new dimension where everything one has left behind is preserved in one's new outlook. We will explore it in more detail in the next four chapters.

The language of the grid

As the revelation people experience on entering 'radically new' suggests, the journey we have just taken through the minds of those inhabiting the six boxes of the grid has not produced a set of accurate descriptions of their partners. They are just impressions, and the only way to corroborate them is to ask partners whether they are true, and the only way to treat the answers is to accept them as true, from their point of view.

The value of the Partnering Grid lies not in the precision of its descriptions, nor the unique truths it reveals, but in the language it provides for the dialogue and discussion that can improve understanding.

In Part II we will explore the language of the grid further by looking at the meanings it gives to the words 'strategy', 'communication', 'leadership', 'trust' and 'conflict'.

Story from the front: use of symbols

When a major UK National Health Service (NHS) trust entered into a partnership to outsource facilities management, it was not looking for a cheap solution to a short-term problem. The trust was looking for a style of partnership that could develop new ways of working together to the partners' mutual advantage.

Committed to this new idea of partnership, the trust used the Partnering Grid to screen potential partners. From its own 'do and review' plot, it found one prospective partner's 'radically new' plot attractive because it seemed to offer opportunities for improved services.

To build a better picture of where the two partners perceived themselves to be on the Partnering Grid, they were asked at the beginning of the partnership to bring some artefact to a meeting that would symbolize how they thought of themselves. The facilities management company's team brought a condom, to symbolize their view of themselves as 'safe but exciting'.

Twelve months on, the partnership was successful, but not extraordinarily so: it had failed to bring about the degree of service enhancement first hoped for. Once more the parties gathered, artefacts in hand, this time to try and understand their inability to implement more radical – and profitable – service offerings. This time, the outsourcing partner brought a lemon, explaining that they felt 'we're being squeezed', and it was clear to the trust that their original 'radically new' position had slipped down the grid to 'arm's length'.

As with all deliberations inspired by the grid, conversations matter more than grid mappings. The value lies not so much in knowing where you are, but rather in talking candidly about how you got there. Improving 'fit' requires each side to understand the dynamics of the shift in perception, so they can act together more effectively in future.

The way the facilities management firm saw it, a year of being browbeaten by lawyers had forced them to abandon their ambitions and move to a cooler 'arm's length' relationship.

Shifts in ownership and affiliation on both sides had reduced early high levels of trust, and as a result ideas that could have resulted in breakthrough services were not being shared among the partners. The trust's insistence on measuring their partner's performance in terms of inputs rather than outputs had also reduced their partner's readiness to adjust resource allocation on their own account to improve service output for the customer. Instead, they felt obliged to concentrate their efforts on complying with the requirements of an increasingly accurate measurement of input costs.

During the anniversary meeting, that lemon concentrated minds wonderfully on ways in which the partnership's processes and measurement systems might be changed to encourage the pursuit of the partnership's original ambitions.

Summary

Partnering success requires a good 'fit' between grid position and 'context'.

By 'context' we mean the external environment, the distribution of power and knowledge, and the partnership's objectives.

A lack of fit requires movement in the grid.

Movement in the grid is a mental act, inspired by changes in perceptions and behaviour.

Left to themselves, partnerships tend to gravitate towards the bottom left or the bottom right of the grid.

How one partner perceives another depends on which box each occupies.

References

Bleeke, J. and Ernst, D. (1995) 'Is your strategic alliance really a sale?', *Harvard Business Review*, January/February.

De Bono, E. (1985) *Six Thinking Hats: The Power of Focused Thinking*, Harmondsworth: Penguin.

Part II
Acting on common ground

5 Living with difference

There has always been a trade-off between creativity and the unity of organizations, but it has become a serious management dilemma only recently, because it is only recently that the turbulence of the environment has reached the point at which creativity and responsiveness have become very desirable and, in some cases, vitally necessary qualities.

In their quest for creativity, organizations have become more trusting: they have made business units more autonomous, and eagerly embraced the idea of 'empowerment'. The policies have worked in many cases – creativity has increased – but before long the newly independent businesses and 'empowered' people have proven unworthy of trust, and begun to pursue objectives different from and in conflict with those of the parent.

Dismayed by the loss of unity and the feeling that things are getting out of hand, many managers have decided that the cost of the improvement in creativity has been too high, and that the autonomy and empowerment must be constrained in some way if unity is to be restored. But then the pendulum swings too far the other way, and the organization becomes locked in a perpetual oscillation between creativity through trust, and unity through control, because the more eagerly the one is pursued, the more attractive the other becomes.

The fear of fragmentation on the one hand and the desire for creativity on the other have led to the idea that the secret is to empower business units and individuals to act on their own initiatives, but only within the constraints of a strong culture and a unifying vision. Empowerment becomes a bargain between leader and led. 'You can have your freedom,' says the leader, 'if you declare your allegiance to my vision. You're not empowered in a general sense. You're empowered to help me realize my dream.'

It is this 'conditional' form of empowerment that creates the problem of 'buy-in'. If empowerment is to be limited, people must agree to its limitations, and a great deal of management – and particularly leadership – effort must therefore be devoted to 'selling' the vision to those whose power it constrains.

This process, which some consultants call 'mobilization', can be prolonged and frustrating, and often leads to competitively disadvantageous delays in implementation. The usual response, however, is to seek faster and more effective 'mobilization' techniques, not to abandon the goal of an integrated view and recognize the multiplicity of individual agendas.

The trouble is that these strenuous efforts to achieve 'buy-in' are seldom successful. When the right view must always be the leadership's view, those who cannot or will not 'get with the programme', or who 'toe the line' instead of 'buying-in', are disenfranchised, feel disempowered, and so behave in ways that frustrate the achievement of the leadership's objectives.

The assumption is that there is only one right view, and since it is impossible in large organizations to get everyone to agree on what that view is, true empowerment ends as soon as efforts to achieve 'buy-in' begin. And the fault when 'buy-in' is not achieved is the individual's, not the leader's, because 'buying-in' is an individual act of commitment.

Those who take a systems view of organizations will say that the failure to achieve 'buy-in' is often the result of a failure to understand the system. But if, as we suggested in Chapter 3, social systems such as business organizations are too complex ever to be 'knowable', attempts to integrate different views into a single view are doomed to failure, and boil down to no more than an insistence that everyone should see the system the leader sees, and help realize the leader's vision of what the system should become.

In many contexts this is a perfectly appropriate strategy, but there are circumstances, in certain industries and at certain times (and in many industries, the present is such a time), when creativity and flexibility are far too important to risk destroying them by trying to impose 'official' visions. These risks are particularly acute in partnerships, because efforts to achieve cross-boundary 'buy-in' are tantamount to attempted cultural colonization, and the destruction of the 'Difference Engine'.

Multiple visions

Suppose for a moment that there is no objective reality, and that what seems to you to be true is just one of many truths that can be perceived by a group of people contemplating the same picture or strategic predicament. You do not have to believe your truth is no better than those of others – you just have to try to imagine what it would be like to run, lead or work within an organization where there is no objective truth, and where your view of what is, and of what can or should be done, is no better than anyone else's.

This thought experiment will be familiar to those who have explored the full philosophical implications of empowerment, because they will have realized that to espouse empowerment is to accept that people should be under no pressure or obligation to adopt the views of others.

It will be objected that such total empowerment is impossible because of the story of the six blind men who were asked to touch an elephant and guess what it was: the first touched a leg, and said it was a tree; the second touched the tail, and said it was a rope; the third touched a flank, and said it was a wall; the fourth touched the trunk, and said it was a snake; the fifth touched a tusk, and said it was a branch, and the sixth touched a toe, and said it was a stone. There is a need for someone with a vision of the whole, it will be argued, that interprets and pieces together the six impressions, to form 'elephant'. It is this kind of reasoning that leads many organizations to constrain local freedoms for the sake of global visions, and diligently seek 'buy-in'.

But is there is another way for the blind men to deduce from their tactile impressions the presence of an elephant? If we are bound by our promise to value every perception of reality equally, what can we do to help the blind men see?

We could help them to develop a language, to communicate with each other, for one thing; we could tell them a bit about the evolution of mammals and of present-day zoology, and we could urge them to listen carefully and use their sense of smell.

Pooh Bear was not the brightest of mammals, but he had a rough idea of what 'hefalumps' were (they were large and liked honey) even though he never actually saw one. And Piglet knew a hefalump when he saw one: it was noisy and it looked like a bear with its head stuck in an empty jar of honey.

Equipped with enough knowledge, the blind men can conceive of an elephant, and if they share a language, they can pool their sense impressions and deduce the presence of an elephant. Their perceptions of the particular elephant they are touching will not be the same, of course, and nor will they correspond exactly with the elephant a sighted person would see, but there will be a lot of overlap between the impressions, which may create enough common ground for a working consensus about what could or should be done, given that elephants exist and that one is close by.

Given the alternative, this strategy for handling differences of view and opinion is worth considering, even by those who reject the idea of a subjective reality. The trouble with the conventional belief that reality is objective and that it is the leaders' job to perceive it and to convince others of the unique validity of their perceptions is that, even if it were true, achieving 'buy-in' is too difficult and takes too long.

If you have to wait until everyone has been either persuaded or fired before you can act, you will probably be too late. It is surely far better to acknowledge that people have their differences, to focus on what unites them, map out the common ground which exists now, and act on it immediately.

When speed is of the essence, the only consensus that one can afford to wait for is the minimum consensus needed to act.

Acting without conviction

Companies that reject 'buy-in' programmes in favour of acting on common ground immediately are faster, more agile and more responsive than those that assume universal conviction is an essential prerequisite for action. They are also very different in other ways.

They receive as well as transmit, because they are profoundly interested in the views and aspirations of all their members, and their efforts are devoted not to changing people, but to changing how they relate to each other.

They sometimes have strong leaders, but it is not a tyrannical strength, impatient with dissent. It is a strength that allows others to define their own realities and provides processes for enabling people to see others' points of view. The emphasis is not on visions, but on relationships, and people recognize that their identities consist of their relationships, and that what they can do and see is governed by context (we will return to the subject of leadership in Chapter 8).

Such organizations acknowledge, for example, that the role of women in society will not be significantly different until there are new spaces in the social fabric for women to be different within. Behavioural change is inspired not by visions, but by perceptions of new opportunities and possibilities. In the same way, collective action occurs when people who are allowed to feel independent recognize their interdependence and see what they can do together. In this way the paradox can be resolved and organizations can be diverse, empowered *and* united.

But this is not the conventional kind of unity that comes from a complete alignment of 'hearts and minds', where everyone is 'singing from the same hymn-sheet'. It is an adequate unity – a sufficiency of shared purpose that also accommodates individual purposes. This modest but practical kind of shared purpose emerges from an environment that allows everyone to contribute, learn from each other, and see that, beyond all their differences, there is common ground on which they can act together for their own and the collective benefit.

If a partnership in which power and knowledge are very widely distributed is none the less active and successful, it is safe to assume that it has accumulated significant amounts of the 'social capital' of trust. But it is not the trust that comes from kinship ties or a shared culture.

Discovering the common ground

The dynamic of any organization is the dynamic of its common ground: the place where individual dreams meet, interact and negotiate a generally desirable common future, and then agree to take steps towards it. If there is no common ground, or if it exists but is not discovered and mapped, there will be no common future, and there will be calls for 'strong' leadership in the conventional sense.

To exploit the dynamic of the common ground, therefore, it is necessary to define it and cultivate an atmosphere of mutual learning that allows the organization and its members to make sense of the past, to understand the present, to adapt to the changes in context, to negotiate through dialogue and to act.

The trouble with this prescription is that it is very hard to cultivate such an atmosphere because, most of the time, most people are locked into their own specialist 'discourses', such as finance, design, marketing, production and personnel, that are more or less unintelligible to those in other discourses.

Somehow or other, a switch must be found to disconnect us from our familiar everyday discourses, and oblige us to find a way of talking and negotiating that is intelligible to everyone. Without such a language, the common ground where trust grows will remain patchy, infertile and largely invisible.

A combination of the Partnering Grid and disciplined dialogue based on the grid can generate such a language, and move the partnership to the strange extremity on the grid that we call 'Radically New'.

We will investigate the 'strategic' implications of 'radically new' in Chapter 6, present a 'communications philosophy' for 'radically new' in Chapter 7, and consider the implications for leadership in Chapter 8.

Summary

The desire for control on the one hand and the need for creativity on the other is one of the central management dilemmas of our time.

The usual solution is to 'empower' people, and achieve 'buy-in' to strong visions at the same time.

A better approach is to abandon the effort to achieve 'buy-in', accept that people see the world differently, and search instead for 'common ground'.

The full power of the 'Difference Engine' is only available on the common ground that appears when independent people recognize their interdependence, and see what they can do together.

6 Exploring common ground

At a concert in Athens, two violinists, one white, one black, one male, one female, stood up and played an improvised duet. The rest of the orchestra and the conductor remained seated. The stage belonged to the violinists.

The music was marvellous – fast, precise and passionate – but it was made doubly exciting by the communication between the two musicians. Neither opened their mouth, but their eyes and expressions, and the rhythmic swaying of their bodies, were eloquent testimony to the richness of their conversation. As the initiative switched from one to the other according to an intuitive cueing system invisible to all but themselves, the audience could see them constantly delighting, surprising and challenging each other to outdo the other's virtuosity and inventiveness with new and ever wilder variations. She began plucking, and he took up the pizzicato with no audible break; he began to bow faster and higher, and then it was she playing faster and higher still.

At times they appeared to be co-operating, and at times they appeared to be competing. The smiles and the warmth of the looks they exchanged suggested they were sharing a peak experience, and knew the music they were making together was better than either could have made on their own.

At the end, the applause was rapturous.

Doubtless the duet could have been recorded, transcribed into musical notation and then performed again, but the act of its creation was quite spontaneous. It was not an expression of a score, or of a conductor's interpretation: it 'emerged' from a space consisting of a stage, respect for and faith in each other's skill, trust in each other's musical instincts, and a shared hunger to create something extraordinary their fellow musicians would admire and their audience would applaud.

It emerged also from a shared professional background and a shared love of music and of the violin. They were musicians, fluent in the language of music and of their instrument. They were acting on common ground rich in possibilities.

They did not know what it would turn out like beforehand, but they shared a set of conventions within a shared language, and they knew the 'space' was full of opportunity and they would not get such a chance again to transcend themselves before an audience in the shadow of the Parthenon (Yanni, 1994).

The poverty of conventional strategy

The trouble with a strategy is that it is a plan, and when the environment is changing fast, plans soon become prisons. When the enterprise is a partnership, plans can become liabilities, because the control that must be exercised to pursue them and keep them on track can lead not just to internal frustration or resentment, but to the destruction of the enterprise.

For this reason, we believe that 'intentional' long-term strategies are ineffective and potentially dangerous in the 'radically new' type of partnership, where difference is valued and the relationship takes priority over the direction.

Some argue that although the extreme volatility of the modern environment requires strategy to be flexible, all enterprises (including partnerships) need a 'sense of direction' before they can act. According to this view, general strategic guidelines are essential if the enterprise is not to wander around aimlessly, achieving nothing.

There is some merit in this argument, but we believe that the necessary 'sense of direction' already exists in partnerships that have identified 'common ground'; that the only strategic guidelines that are needed are those represented by all the different overlapping possibilities, perceptions, ambitions, premonitions, competencies and imaginations of which 'common ground' largely consists.

The two violinists at the Acropolis lacked even a rudimentary score. Their plan was merely to improvise, and their sense of direction came from themselves and their setting – from where they were, who they were, what they could do, their knowledge of each other's personality and talent, and their wish to make good use of the opportunity they had to display their art.

If 'strategy' means a deliberate intent, embedded in detailed, long-term plans, then strategy is close to its sell-by date. There is still room for a humbler kind of short-term project planning in a 'radically new' partnership, but the place of the planning usually associated with the word 'strategy' is taken by a spontaneous searching process that can be characterized as the 'exploration of common ground'.

It is the same throughout business. What management theorists proclaim as inspired strategies, adeptly implemented, usually turn out on closer inspection to be the creations of lucky accidents or chance encounters. Many of the textbook cases of 'brilliant' business strategies of recent years are rationalizations after the event that only seem to be intentional strategies in retrospect. The well-known case of Honda's entry into the US market (it intended to sell motorcycles, but the Americans were much more interested in the mopeds its salespeople used) illustrates the key role serendipity plays in many successful so-called 'strategies'.

Strategy and the grid

The grid in strategic mode is shown in Figure 6.1. Its six boxes map the six perceptions of partnership shown in Table 6.1.

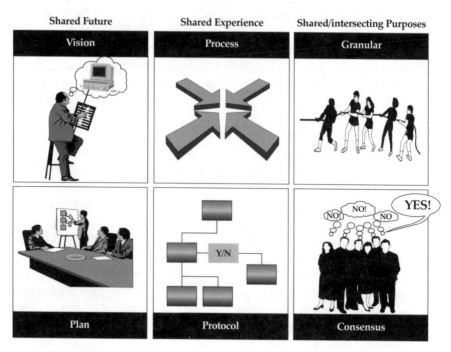

Figure 6.1   Strategy grid

Table 6.1   Strategy grid

Perception of partnership	Perception of strategy
'Command and control'	Plan
'Hearts and minds'	Vision
'Arm's length'	Protocol
'Do and review'	Process
'Gridlock'	Consensus
'Radically new'	Granular

Let us look at the six boxes in Figure 6.1 in a little more detail.

Bottom left

In 'command and control', a strategy is a long-term intent that takes precedence over everything and everyone. The future has a special status here, and is assumed to be malleable. It is encapsulated in written plans of great perceived potency, to which all must contribute. There is usually a strategic plan, drafted by an individual or a small planning group, and an implementation plan drafted later. Predictability and control are both seen as essential qualities of the planning process, and it is taken for granted that a faithful implementation of the plan will bring about the desired outcomes.

Consider the case of a large engineering firm which formed a small team to look ahead and suggest ways in which it could maximize its survival chances in an increasingly competitive market.

One of the main ideas to emerge was a major restructuring of the company, involving many new lines of interaction between individuals and teams, and thus the formation of a host of new internal and external relationships or partnerships. The team spent six months shut away in a Portakabin gathering data and dreaming up ideas. The analysis was exemplary, the problems were well understood, the detail was precisely documented, but the ideas were the ideas of engineers – elegant, precise, low-tolerance. They took no account at all of the fact that their application would substantially change the working lives of a large number of people. People were seen as components.

When this was pointed out by someone from a different part of the company, the planners realized they had more work to do. Rather than gathering information from the hitherto neglected components, however, they set about planning how to implement their plan. Eight months into the project, most employees were unaware of their existence.

Top left

In 'hearts and minds', the 'strategic intent' takes the form of an inspiring vision, but the focus remains firmly on a shared future. Strategy formation remains the responsibility of top management, but far more effort is made to win the commitment of those affected by it. Written documents are important here, too, but they take the form not of plans, but of visions and statements of mission, value and guiding principles.

In addition, leaders often embark on company-wide road-shows, consisting of presentations, question-and-answer sessions and so-called 'town meetings' at every site, to spread the gospel of the new vision and urge people to exert themselves in its pursuit. The 'envisioning' process relies heavily on will and intention, and the implementation process is seen as a matter of doing what is needed to get from 'as is' to 'to be'.

The leaders of one large company decided that their vision of the future could only be realized if everyone subscribed to and always acted in accordance with five 'core values'. Much time and considerable sums in consultancy fees were spent on selecting and drafting the values, which were then printed on small plastic cards issued to employees. Thousands of larger copies were also made and distributed for public display.

One of the authors was walking through the company's accounts department when she spotted a 'core value' poster stuck up on a wall, next to the photocopier. The third core value was 'We respect each other,' but someone had crossed out the first two letters of the second word and replaced them with 'su'. There is always another view.

Bottom middle

In 'arm's length', the past is more important, because it is the source of the shared experiences from which partners derive their rules of interaction, or protocols. The emphasis is not on where they are going, but on the way they take each step.

Clear norms of interaction are established, and much effort is devoted to scanning the environment for information about how to improve the quality of interactions within the established norms. Strategic plans and implementation programmes usually take the form of a sequence of steps or phases.

For instance, European Economic and Monetary Union (EMU) is the next logical step in the process of European integration. There are clear criteria for entry, and there is a clear procedure for implementing EMU once the countries' candidacies have been approved. The trouble is that there is a large and diverse group of parties to the proposed union that are threatening to derail it. Right-wingers in Britain oppose EMU because they are worried about 'sovereignty'; the French labour unions are against it because they object to the tough economic policies needed to ensure France meets the entry criteria, and in Germany, at the time of writing, many are fearful that the EMU entry criteria will be relaxed to such an extent that the common currency, the euro, will lack the strength of the Deutschmark, in which they take such pride.

Europeans have so far proved very tolerant of the differences that divide them, but the EMU project has already shown there are limits to their toleration, and that apart from those who have staked their political reputations on the integration of Europe, there is no major constituency that really values the differences between the European Union's member states.

Top middle

Shared experiences are also the inspiration of strategy in 'do and review', but in this case the partnering protocols become processes that are always under review. As in 'arm's length', the future and 'strategy' are less important than what can be learned from what has already happened.

Past experience is the inspiration of strategy here, too, but strategic 'input' is gathered more widely, particularly from front-line or 'customer-facing' staff, and efforts are made to achieve a broader alignment of objectives, to ensure that the relationship continues after current projects are completed.

There is a sense in this box that the partnership itself has 'a right to life', and thus its own strategic momentum.

After a consultancy had completed a major 'logistics' project for a specialist retailer, it felt, as is often the case with difficult projects, that it had learned quite a bit about its client's business. So the consultants' project team asked for a meeting with the client's CEO to discuss other possibilities.

As a result of that and subsequent meetings at various levels of the two organizations, a joint venture company was formed, to offer the solution to non-competing retailers with similar system requirements. The joint venture already has two satisfied clients, and talks are now in progress on extending its range of services.

Bottom right

In 'gridlock', strategy becomes fuzzier, and action is informed by mutual understanding (or rather, inhibited by the lack of it).

The present looms larger than the past or the future, because it is accepted that the destinies of the partners are linked, and all that is left is to decide what to do next within the common ground that has been mapped out. Strategy emerges as a series of projects, from regular meetings, and much effort is devoted to ensuring that there is something for everyone.

But areas of potential difficulty or friction are avoided, so they tend to grow until the partnership becomes trapped in a state of inertia, where survival becomes the main objective.

This drift to inertia was evident at a women's conference in a public sector service organization, where 70 delegates from different levels and functions were discussing the future of the women's forum and other related issues. The objective of the conference was to allow everyone to hear the many different perspectives on the positions of women in the service, and to agree a way forward. In order to ensure a 'safe' space for women to discuss those matters of particular importance to them, men (who occupied many positions of power in the service) were not invited.

Proposals for change were therefore framed within the context of what was currently possible, and moreover, a strong culture of consensus was shared by many delegates. Although there was much passionate talk about democracy and many demands for an equal voice, the desire for consensus soon led to a collusion of the powerless to keep things as they were. When it came to agreeing on actions for change, one group who were holding up the hierarchy from beneath were unable to make any decisions about priorities and practicality, for fear of alienating any member of their group.

When combined with the absence of significant, powerful voices from across the organization, this fear of 'rocking the boat'

effectively prevented the discussion of any potential futures significantly different from those that were already obvious: name-
ly those where the women continued to feel powerless. The inertia in the system thus supported the status quo.

Top right

In 'radically new', partners understand that what matters is not
how well they understand each other, but what they are already
willing and able to do. The present dominates both right-hand
boxes, but in 'radically new', much greater efforts are made to
understand and map the common ground from which 'doable'
projects emerge.

Continual updating of information about the environment
and about the widest possible range of individual aspirations is a
distinctive feature of such relationships. The strategy is not
'intended'; it emerges from the projects that themselves emerge
from the wide-ranging conversations among the constantly
widening partnership community.

At the time of writing, we are setting up a new joint research
project with a group of partner organizations to explore in more
depth some of the issues raised by our work to date. In view of
the vital role played by the distribution of power in determining
the nature and creativity of relationships, all the members have
chosen to abandon traditional ownership. Instead, the whole
group has co-designed activities in such a way that power, knowledge, purpose and thus any value created are also distributed.

In the first working meeting with the core members, the issue
of strategy in distributed communities was discussed at some
length, thereby providing the space to address the group's survival and sustainability. This is not as straightforward as it might
seem, because conversations are always started by an individual.
This inevitably 'positions' the initiator as a proposer and obliges
other members of the group to respond to the proposal, either by
rejecting it or 'buying-in' to it.

There was an almost palpable shift of emphasis, from 'buy-in'
to 'collaboration', when we all faced the fact that survival was
not guaranteed and that it was up to us to work together to give
it life.

A strong sense of commitment emerged from this meeting, which we attributed to the group's success in mapping out patterns of current and future conversations, which would keep all our separate ideas and actions interrelated in a 'collaborative' space.

The conventional 'buy-in' model would have led us down a safe and predictable path. The model we have chosen has opened up 'common ground' that is already alive with a host of possible projects and alliances, from knowledge creation to commercial applications, the complexity and richness of which could not have been seen, let alone explored and co-ordinated, had the partnership been 'managed' from a single perspective.

Emergent strategy

We call 'radically new' strategy 'granular' because it is not a 'strategy', in the conventional sense, but rather a series of projects. In 'radically new', strategy emerges. It is not intended. There is no conventional strategy, but when common ground is found by people with a propensity to act, it can produce something so good and in tune with the times that it seems afterwards as if it must have been planned. It is like scientific research, where outcomes are unknown and unknowable and the only goal is to 'break new ground'.

All partnerships, including those we call 'radically new', need some stability to prevent them from falling apart, but in the 'radically new' partnership, the stabilizing part of the system is being constantly challenged.

All modern organizations are battlegrounds where the official and the formal are fighting to the death with the subversive and the disorganized. In traditional integrated organizations, there is usually enough central power to keep the subversive systems at bay. 'Radically new' partnerships lack such central power, and are thus more open to challenge, more vulnerable to shadow conspiracies, and therefore less stable.

Most writers see this instability as a weakness. We do not; on the contrary, we see it as unavoidable in a partnership where difference is valued, and a source of considerable strength in circumstances where creativity and an ability to innovate are at a premium.

Ralph Stacey (1996) insists it is only when an organization is both stable and unstable at the same time that it generates new forms of behaviour and can innovate. He says the creative process 'is inevitably messy', and that 'to remove the mess, by inspiring us to follow some common vision, share the same culture and pull together, is to remove ... the raw material of creative activity'.

The fact that 'radically new' partnerships cannot be controlled does not mean they are anarchic. Their sense of shared destiny and their common ground together *contain* (rather than remove) their characteristic instability, and are the context for the emergence of granular strategy (see Chapter 8 for more on the important idea of 'containment'). Stacey says the human need to 'belong' and 'to sustain the support of others is a very powerful form of control', but is exerted not by an individual, but by the group as a whole. 'There is control, but no one is "in control".'

A 'radically new' partnership is an example of what complexity scientists call a 'complex adaptive system'. Although such systems are always on the edge of chaos, they display ordered patterns of behaviour. These patterns cannot be contrived, and their detailed consequences cannot be predicted, but they can maintain a partnership's balance on the edge of instability.

Structure as strategy

As the partnership moves across the grid from left to right, power becomes less centralized, the 'shape' of the enterprise becomes more fluid and changeable, action is more spontaneous and harder to direct, and 'strategic' decision-making becomes increasingly difficult. One could say that in partnerships on the left of the grid, strenuous and largely successful efforts are made to emulate the 'tightness' of traditional enterprise architectures, and that it is only when partnerships start to tolerate and value difference that they achieve architectural novelty and the constrained instability from which creativity emerges.

Some argue that structure *is* strategy, and modern competition consists not, as is usually supposed, of a strategic, but of a structural 'arms race', in which firms vie with each other to design more 'creative' enterprise architectures. According to Gianni Lorenzoni of the University of Bologna, in Italy, and Charles Baden-Fuller, of the University of Bath, in England, one of the most striking developments in business in recent years has been the sudden emergence of what they call 'tight networks' as powerful competitors to conventional, integrated enterprises (Lorenzoni and Baden-Fuller, 1995).

They say that tight networks were operating when Apple worked with Adobe and Canon to develop a laser-jet printer, and Corning linked its glass-making to BICC's cable-making expertise to produce optical fibres. They claim it was the 'tight network' structure of Sun Systems that enabled the US workstation firm to boost sales and profits from zero in 1982 to $3.2 billion and $284 million respectively in ten years, and achieve value-added per employee figures that were the envy of its rivals.

Lorenzoni and Baden-Fuller say that Apple, Nintendo (video games), Corning (medical and optical products) and Genentech (genetic engineering and biotechnology) have demonstrated the power of the 'tight network' in technology-driven industries; McKesson has used it to good effect in the distribution of drugs; Ikea and Body Shop have shown the leverage it offers in retailing; McDonald's have won market leadership in fast food with it, and 'tight network' structures have supercharged the growth of Benetton and Nike. They say that 'tight networks' are also proving formidable competitors in the banking, airline, hotel and management consulting sectors.

The roles they assign to the 'central firm', and the emphasis they place on shared visions and cultural compatibility, show the Lorenzoni/Baden-Fuller 'tight network' is still some way from the 'Radically New' box in our grid, but much of what they say about 'tight networks' resonates well with the 'radically new' philosophy.

They point out that the central firms rely on non-contractual glue to bind networks together, because they know that formal contracts covering every eventuality reduce flexibility and erode the cost advantage which makes the network competitive. They say that central firms always exercise their power with care, because if it was used in arbitrary or self-serving ways, the network could split.

The democratic nature of 'tight networks' is reflected in their distributions of economic power. Many McDonald's and Benetton franchisees, for example, earn higher returns on capital than their central firms. The aim of a central firm is not to grab the lion's share of reward, but to keep the network united.

Private information is anathema in the 'tight network'. Members exchange not only data, but also ideas, feelings and hunches about market trends. Nike invites its network partners to its Beaverton research laboratory, to show them new developments in materials, design, technology and markets, and Toyota subcontractors receive training from their central firm.

Structure affects the quality of information because within a hierarchical, integrated structure, knowledge is often power, and tends to be transmuted as it is transmitted. In a 'tight network', knowledge is a common resource. It flows freely, and is untainted by its role as a currency of power.

But Lorenzoni and Baden-Fuller warn that the development of a true information-sharing culture is far from easy. They found a number of cases in which alliances failed because partners abused their information-sharing privileges. In one case, the delinquent member used network information as an entry ticket to a rival alliance. It is thus risky for a member of a 'tight network' to be open with information, and it will be reluctant to take the risk in the absence of trust and a commitment to reciprocity.

It is in the area of trust where 'radically new' partnerships part company with 'tight networks'. Trust is a prerequisite in a 'tight network', because without it nothing can be done. In a 'radically new' partnership, where 'knowledge' is in the eye of the local beholder and power is widely distributed, trust is a quality that grows as mutually rewarding joint projects are completed. The exigencies of the shared tasks create the need to hear other views and to share knowledge. Trust is not some grand, transcendent ethos that stems from a joint commitment to a shared vision, because there *is* no shared vision in the 'radically new' partnership. It is a more humble and practical quality that improves the effectiveness of communication, and helps to extend the common ground (see Chapter 9).

The next step

A 'tight network' is similar to, but not quite the same as, what we mean by a 'radically new' partnership. The main difference is that in a 'radically new' partnership there is no permanent central firm. A member of the partnership who takes the lead in one particular project will be happy to play a supporting role in another. There is no fixed centre; the centre moves to the network node best equipped to lead the project at hand.

As we have seen, strategy is not intended in 'radically new' partnerships; it emerges from the 'common ground', and by and large it takes a granular form, consisting of a series of more or less discrete projects.

The impetus to undertake particular projects emerges from the common ground, and the permanent *frisson* of anxiety that runs through organizations balanced on the edge of instability. If people are anxious but confident in their own abilities and those of their partners, they will want to be doing things.

What they will want to do will be determined by how well they know each other, because this determines the richness and the extent of the partnership's common ground. Although the total 'opportunity set' is defined by the 'hinterlands' of all the partners (the competences, networks and dreams they bring with them to the common ground), the proportion of the opportunity set that is accessible depends crucially on the connectivity between these hinterlands. In other words, the more intimate members are with the abilities, networks and dreams of their partners, the more opportunities they will spot, and the more energetic, creative and adaptable the partnership will be.

In Chapter 7 we will discuss how a partnership can use the techniques of dialogue to enrich and extend its access to its opportunity set. For the moment, it is enough to note that it is this interplay between the hinterlands of partners that inspires a series of projects which, looking back, sometimes seems to have been a strategy.

There is 'intention' here, but only in the form of the dreams and aspirations of individuals. 'Strategy', in the usual sense of the word, is a personal thing: it is the rubbing together of these individual life-plans that generates and guides the partnership's actions, not intentional partnership strategy.

A 'radically new' partnership moves because each of its members wants to take the next step. It is just like the violin duet described at the beginning of this chapter. The partnership 'setting' requires action, but no individual has any idea of where the action will lead. They do their own 'thing', in the context of their knowledge of the 'things' of their partners.

Those who find it difficult to imagine how an enterprise – whether an integrated organization or a partnership – that lacks a 'strategic intent', as Gary Hamel and C.K. Prahalad (1994) called it, can move at all, let alone with any vigour, should consider the case of the British microprocessor intellectual property provider ARM.

ARM's way

Partnering in multiple dimensions

When Cambridge-based Acorn Computers decided to 'spin out' an advanced research and development team in November 1990 to form Advanced RISC Machines (ARM), the fledgling company was faced with a strategic dilemma.

Five years earlier, the part of Acorn that was to become ARM had produced the world's first commercial single-chip RISC (Reduced Instruction Set Computer) processor, which made its first appearance in Acorn's Archimedes personal computer in 1987. Later versions of this same processor are still used in Acorn's RISC PC today.

From the beginning, the ARM processors were designed to offer high performance at low cost. The ARM team then realized the value of the low power consumption of these early chips (they did not need fans, and batteries lasted longer), and optimized later designs for energy efficiency.

The dilemma was the mismatch between ARM's resources and the huge market for small, fast, energy-efficient chips that were easy to programme and had very good 'code density' (they need less memory for a particular programme than competing RISCs, and so reduce system costs).

In the semiconductor industry, the traditional way to exploit such a technological lead is to raise a pile of money and become an integrated design, development, manufacturing and marketing company. When Robin Saxby was interviewed for the job of ARM's CEO, he proposed a different approach. 'We started with £1.75 million,' he recalls, '£1.5 million from Apple, £250 000 from VLSI, and Acorn's intellectual property. My idea was to run very lean and very quickly, and get into profit fast. We had outstanding people, a leading architecture and the chance to transform it from an Acorn into a global standard, but we didn't have the capital for manufacturing.'

Partnership was central to Saxby's plan. He saw ARM's essence as the design and development of RISC processors and systems, and he was going to stick to that. Everything else needed to turn ARM chips into world-beaters – software, software tools, systems building, manufacturing, marketing, distribution, etc. – would be provided through a policy Saxby called 'partnering in multiple dimensions'.

ARM did not come to partnering – it was built on it. 'That is the benefit of a clean sheet of paper,' says Saxby. 'We had no history, so we could plan for a "global partnership" from the outset and concentrate on doing what we were best at.'

The shape of ARM's 'global partnership' was determined by its investors, the value chain in the microchip industry, and the market segments its products were best suited for. ARM's investors are Acorn, Apple, chip maker VLSI Technology, NIF (Nippon Investment & Finance; the venture capital arm of Daiwa Securities) and ARM staff. The three trade investors, Acorn, Apple and VLSI, are also ARM partners, but they do not have exclusive rights to ARM technology. In addition to VLSI,

ARM semiconductor partners included another 18 chip makers at the time of writing (June 1997).

ARM licenses its technology to semiconductor partners, who do the manufacturing, applications development and marketing. It selects partners for their technology or systems expertise, so the partnership as a whole provides the marketplace with the widest possible choice of development options within a common RISC platform. 'We can license to anyone we want,' explains Saxby. 'We charge an up-front licensing fee and then a royalty per piece.'

The market segments ARM has identified as most promising are 'portable' (smart phones, Personal Digital Assistants [PDAs], cellular phones, etc.), 'multi-media' (network computers, set-top boxes, digital TVs, etc.), and 'embedded' (in automotive, computer games consoles, mass storage, printers, disk drives, faxes, modems, network controllers, video subsystems, etc.).

Apple backed ARM because it wanted to use ARM-based chips in its Newton PDA; the UK company Psion (the world's leading PDA designer) uses an ARM-based chip in its latest Series 5 hand-held computer; VLSI developed an ARM-based dual-chip design for the European GSM digital cellular phone standard; 3DO's Interactive Multiplayer (made under license by Panasonic, Sanyo, Lucky Goldstar and Creative Labs) employs an ARM-based controller; Oracle's network computer and Eidos's video phone both use ARM-based chip sets, and Online Media has committed itself long-term to ARM chips for its 'set-top boxes' – mass market devices that turn a TV into an interactive multi-media display.

An important non-technical attraction for the consumer goods manufacturer (the embedded market), which seems serendipitous until one recognizes that enterprise structure is enterprise strategy, is that ARM's multiple partnerships make it easier for them to arrange local sources of supply.

Having identified the key market segments, ARM developed what Saxby calls 'roadmaps': product development plans designed to allow the growing band of ARM *aficionados* to design their own product development strategies around specifications for more advanced chips ARM had committed itself to developing. The 'roadmaps' exemplify ARM's partnering philosophy, because they reveal to partners product development information that, in a conventional semiconductor company, would be regarded as highly confidential. Saxby sees it differently. He wants ARM partners to commit long-term to the ARM architecture and, to be willing to do that, he believes they need to know what ARM has 'up its sleeve', so to speak: 'It costs us and our semiconductor partners several million dollars to develop a new chip,' he explains, 'so we have to be sure there are products ready and waiting for it. The network is a model of openness, as well as of partnership.'

Partnership characterizes the firm's research and development (R&D), too. It spends 30% of sales on R&D, often in partnership with universities and other research establishments. As Saxby puts it: 'We recycle intellectual property.' He says that ARM is part of the 'Cambridge *keiretsu*', the affiliation of friends that spawned its erstwhile parent, Acorn, and scores of other high-technology companies that have sprung up around the town.

At the other end of the value chain, the company reserves the right in its licensing agreements to seek its own end user partners and customers, and to 'see through' its semiconductor partners and deal with their customers directly. There is an evangelical aspect to 'selling' a novel architecture, and the best evangelists are those intimate with both the faith and the product development roadmaps: 'We are the keepers of the ARM architecture,' says Saxby. 'We must take care of the main marketing thrust, because our partners are more interested in promoting themselves.'

ARM and a semiconductor partner will often act as a marketing team, to open up new markets such as automotive, where TI and Oki (both ARM partners) are already strong. Saxby says that with the help of its partnership model, ARM can penetrate new markets within two years.

It would be surprising if a firm that has made such a success of such a full-blooded partnering strategy (sales rose from less than £1m in 1991 to over £10m in 1995, and after start-up losses of £2m in the first two years, ARM operating profit topped the £3m mark in 1995) had not learned a thing or two about the art of partnering. We will look at the ARM style of partnering in Chapter 7. For the moment, it is enough to acknowledge that the business model that Saxby outlined at his interview six years ago has been partially corroborated. 'Partnership allows rapid market accept-ance,' he says, 'creates open, global standards and, because of the wider geographical spread it provides, it makes you far less vul-nerable to local economic volatility. It seems to work in the early stages, at least. We're self-funding and cash generating.'

As a growth strategy, it has yet to be proven, but Saxby seems confident that teamwork, networking, joint sales activity and constant innovation, plus some acquisitions of complementary technologies and people, will keep the momentum going.

He expects ARM's way of business to be copied. 'We didn't set out to change the past,' he says, 'we set out to do something for the future. We had to do things differently – to develop an anti-culture – if we were going to be world class. I think we have a great business model.'

A new enterprise model

The ARM story is the best illustration of the 'radically new' per-ception of partnership we have come across. ARM's 'strategy', if one can call it that, is more a creature of its nightmares than of its dreams. It did not want to be a manufacturer, it did not relish going back, cap in hand, to investors for more cash all the time and diluting employees' equity, and above all, it did not want to be gobbled up by a huge corporate bureaucracy that would stifle its creativity and subject its R&D budget to the mercies of across-the-board cost cuts.

ARM 'borrows' its strategy from its partners, especially from the chip manufacturers. It is a node in several distributed enter-prises, active in several markets, and its ultimate fate is entirely in the hands of its partners: software developers and systems designers, as well as chip makers.

It takes pains to explore and understand the hinterlands of all its partners, particularly their customers, which it sees as the cus-tomers of the enterprise of which it is part; and as we shall see, it makes strenuous efforts to communicate on as broad a band-width as possible.

It seems highly unlikely that any of ARM's partners see their own business relationships, including those with ARM, in the same 'radically new' way, but that is of no consequence to ARM. It is happy to work with and adapt to any organization whose interests and competencies are complementary with its own. It selects partners with care, but not on the basis of cultural similarity. It is difference that ARM values most in its many partners, because the more different they are, the more the relationships extend ARM's opportunity set.

ARM's 'radically new' perception of partnership is also evident in its openness – exemplified by its 'roadmaps' – and in the inherently democratic nature of its partnerships. It is not in awe of, or overpowered by, its much larger partners. There are times and situations in which it plays a supporting role, but there are also occasions when its unique know-how makes it the natural leader of a product development or marketing project.

Although it has been positively promiscuous in its partnering so far, it is loyal and sees each relationship as potentially long-term. It has little idea of where each will lead, but is content to take one step at a time, in the hope that the more the 'common ground' is explored, the more opportunity-rich it will become.

Its people are poly-cultural, alert, highly communicative and responsive, and insatiably curious about the hinterlands of the people they deal with. They are willing to take risks, but they question everything, are no respecters of authority, and are hungry for success in joint enterprises where rewards are shared in ways that seem to them to be fair.

They are inspired not by specific business visions, but by a faith in the RISC technology they have mastered, and of which they are the 'keepers', as Robin Saxby puts it. They will go where it leads; they have no wish to plan its life in detail. They are assiduous project planners, of course, but they have no 'strategy', in the conventional sense, apart from the wish not to miss good opportunities, or make mistakes twice, and a determination to maintain their balance in a rapidly changing industry.

Story from the front: SEEBOARD

Following its privatization in 1994, the UK utility SEEBOARD (South East Electricity Board) undertook a restructuring to transform itself from a centralized monopoly to a group of deregulated businesses, interacting within a client–provider framework. Contract management (part of the client side of the business) was charged with the task of developing creative, mutually rewarding partnerships following a history of difficult relationships.

A group from contract management shared with us some of their concerns. They said that for many of those involved, their only previous experience of partnerships was of rigid, one-sided, contract-driven relationships, and that before the restructuring began, there was a lack of trust and choice, a lot of empire-building and sitting on information, a preoccupation with power and how to get it, a general pessimism and a conviction that the past would 'get in the way', much defensiveness and fear of what people saw as an increasingly competitive and volatile marketplace.

The challenge for contract management was to devise new kinds of relationship when no one knew how to do it. How could they cultivate a true partnership culture among people who regarded relationship issues as 'pink and fluffy', and who assumed that all contracts were always 'longer than *War and Peace*' and designed for protection rather than collaboration?

People were content to give away the relationship problems to Human Resources, so that the latter could arrange 'away days' to develop shared cultures and visions, because they knew it had nothing to do with the real work; it was a sideline activity which in some general way was expected to do everybody good.

But, given what they called 'the baggage', people in provider departments were aware of the danger that the new contracts would simply confirm unequal patterns of power in a way that gave contract management the upper hand, and they were anxious to avoid that.

For their part, contract management staff were concerned that the business units, with their negative attitudes, would try to manipulate the situation to their own advantage in ways not covered by the terms of the contract, and so invisible to contract management.

However, most people accepted that such attitudes would be a liability in the new market conditions. They recognized that utilities are equipped to manage monopolies, but not markets, and that they were very good at sticking to the rules – some said that had been the essence of their work until now. They were not optimistic that things could change simply because someone at head office decided to change the rules. They saw partnering as very 'contractual' because that had been their only experience of it, and feared the new contracts would make their relationships inflexible.

Using the Partnering Grid changed the way many people talked about the situation. The provider units saw the contracts as the instruments of a 'command and control' approach that would generate conflict but provide no means of resolving it. They said the 'command and control' approach had worked in the past because conformity had been enforced, but would not work in a client–provider arrangement, where business units were free to develop independently.

They approved of the client–provider system, because they felt their survival chances would be greatly enhanced if different business units developed different styles. But they were worried that since the only mechanism in 'command and control' for managing difficult relationships was enforced uniformity, its retention as the dominant management style would make the restructuring ineffective.

They wanted the business units to be permitted to help design contracts that suited them, but did want not to be obliged to 'buy-in' to some grand vision.

They found the risk management aspects of 'command and control' (by controlling market and partners) attractive, but knew the approach would do nothing to build trust, and would prevent different views and the opportunities associated with them from being seen or heard. (Looking back, some said that had it not been for the partnering discussions, they might well have failed to spot the opportunities that led them to establish a new joint venture with a subcontractor.)

Information was another worry. They feared they would not have enough of it to manage effectively. Bureaucracies are good at managing knowledge centrally; everyone knows where everything is, and it is easy to document and disseminate procedures and best practice. But it was felt that this approach would be counter-productive in the new context because it dealt in dead knowledge, and what they really needed was live knowledge that changed from day to day. They realized that managing knowledge was part of managing the relationship.

So if 'command and control' was inappropriate, the question was: what style of partnering should they adopt? They had tried the 'hearts and minds' approach, and were not prepared to try again.

'We are engineers,' they told us. 'We want you to know that we just don't do "pink and fluffy". We need to get that straight from the start.' 'Hearts and minds' was, for them, too 'pink and fluffy', and it required people to change before they could act together, and there was no time to learn people skills before they got the new structure moving.

They found the notion that people could work together despite being different very liberating, and only invoked the 'pink and fluffy' metaphor whenever they felt they were being asked to be different. They wanted to do things differently, but not to become different sorts of people.

The contract management group asked others in the new system to complete the Partnering Grid and discuss existing attitudes to partnering and partners. They then ran two full-day sessions with business unit managers, others from client services and members of the executive board. The two sessions were focused on real tasks and practical outcomes, rather than on relationship issues *per se*. They were aimed at discovering what would fit into a collective interpretation, and securing commitments to act on the common ground revealed. The result was a series of multi-unit initiatives designed to make the new Power Networks arrangement work for everyone.

In their reflections about their work, people also referred to a number of general changes in their outlook. They realized that consensus was a negotiated and evolving relationship between many different stakeholders, rather than a static consensus fixed at the first sign of agreement.

Previously, there had been one dominant story about SEE-BOARD that was somehow 'truer' than the rest. In spite of the decentralizing objective of the company, this story was often interpreted as if it had come from head office. In fact, of course, it was always a composite of many stories, but what happened during their discussions around partnering was that far more of the stories were shared publicly. The 'one true story' myth could no longer be sustained.

People referred to a 'black book': the official version of what the new organization was and would become. All the managers, from both client and provider units, knew it more or less by heart.

Before the dialogue days, the injunction had been interpreted as: 'Be creative, by the book.' In other words, the new partnerships knew they were being asked to act differently, but were unable to do so because they only knew how to act together according to 'the rules'. Dialogue brought the 'black book' and head office mentality out into the open, and allowed people to see why things were as they were. Once rules are visible and 'on the surface', people can change them, if they want to.

Some people were nervous about revealing such information, but one executive was very relaxed about it, because it was clear to him that his information (which he openly and honestly acknowledged was about control) was part of the system, and no one had asked him to change or (God forbid!) become 'pink and fluffy'. He saw it as a practical way to discover what would happen in the new 'context'.

The point to bear in mind here is that when people discover, through dialogue, that a proposal is deemed to be 'not doable' by the group, it is not the dialogue that prevents it from happening. It could not have happened anyway, but it might have taken far longer to find that out without the dialogue.

Summary

Intentional strategy is ineffective, and can be dangerous in ambitious partnerships.

The nature of strategy differs from grid box to grid box.

In ambitious partnerships, strategy is granular and emerges from the partners' common ground.

The strategy of ARM reflects a 'radically new' approach to partnering.

References

Hamel, G. and Prahalad, C.K. (1994) *Competing for the Future,* Harvard Business School Press.

Lorenzoni, G. and Baden-Fuller, C. (1995) 'Creating a strategic centre to manage a web of partners', *California Management Review,* Spring.

Stacey, R. (1996) *Complexity and Creativity in Organizations,* Berrett-Koehler.

'Yanni at the Acropolis with the Royal Philharmonic Concert Orchestra', (1994), (video), Private Music: distributed by BMG.

7 Trading in 'common' sense

A characteristic feature of 'radically new' is a new philosophy of communications which pervades every medium, from corridor conversations and e-mail chat to video conferences and formal face-to-face meetings.

The reason we need a new philosophy of communications is that the old conventions and habits of business discourse take no account of the power plays and hidden agendas that underlie business and work conversations and prevent important matters from being discussed, leading to serious misunderstandings and missed opportunities, and provide no basis for selecting what medium of interaction to use.

The problem of power plays is illustrated by Shaw's fictional exchange between Napoleon and Guiseppe:

Napoleon: What shall I do with this soldier, Guiseppe? Everything he says is wrong.
Guiseppe: Make him a general, excellency, and then everything he says will be right.

As Chris Blantern of the UK consultancy Re-View has pointed out, Guiseppe was describing an attitude to knowledge that is just as common, if not more so, in the modern world as it was in Napoleon's time. Because we can never know enough to know what 'the truth' is, we tend to attribute veracity to views, descriptions, encyclicals, statements and observations on the basis of the pedigree of the source.

Blantern (1997) claims that whether or not we are conscious of doing so, we all apply the following tests (in descending order of legitimacy) to putative 'knowledge' when deciding whether or not to believe it:

- From how 'high' has it descended (the higher the better)?
- How 'expert' is the source (the more expert the better)?
- Does the source have social status (the more socially acceptable and 'politically correct' the better)?
- Does the source have practical status (is he or she orthodox and realistic, or esoteric and 'off the wall')?
- What is my previous experience of 'knowledge' from this source (did it turn out to be 'true')?
- Does the knowledge fit with my current experience?
- Is the knowledge corroborated by others?

There is so much information around nowadays that we are more or less obliged to delegate the mammoth task of reducing it to digestible quantities to 'experts' (newspaper editors and TV commentators). We do not have the time or qualifications to do it ourselves.

But it is not just broadcast media that are intermediated in this way. Many face-to-face conversations, including business and work meetings, are so tainted by politics, prejudice, false assumptions and unwarranted inferences that even this richest of all media is woefully inefficient and ineffective at a time when efficient and effective business communication has never been so important.

What can be done to improve the quality of business talk so that it becomes more efficient and effective?

The first thing we can do is to acknowledge that knowledge is not what it was. In the past, most of what was known could be known unequivocally, in a scientific way. As we have already noted, a growing amount of what masquerades as 'truth' is not really truth at all, but opinion and point of view. Although some of what we do in business can still be based on 'facts', much of what we do has to be done on the basis of information that is inherently equivocal.

Blantern says that 'knowledge is a local and a social phenomenon', influenced by time, place, function, culture and the personal agendas of people with the power, like Guiseppe's general, to make their views official.

It is not practical or even possible to get at the 'truth' in these inherently equivocal areas, or to cleanse conversations of all of their contaminants. It is possible, however, to get more of the 'situation' – particularly the hidden agendas and private assumptions that inspire people to talk and behave in the ways they do – out into the open.

Figure 7.1 embodies our belief that interactions between people are best seen as forms of trade in power, knowledge and meaning.

On the left-hand side of the grid, where power and knowledge are both concentrated, people trade power according to rules of interaction that either are taken for granted (in the case of 'command and control') or are embedded and largely hidden in the culture (in the case of 'hearts and minds').

In the middle of the grid, where power is still concentrated but knowledge is relatively widely distributed, people trade knowledge in ways that are managed in the interest of process improvement, in 'arm's length' or in ways that invite people to participate in developing the partnership within the overall strategic framework set out by the leadership oligarchy in 'do and review'.

In both cases, knowledge is generally seen as a commodity – a common resource that can be accumulated, processed, organized and managed centrally, and then dealt in and talked about in a common language.

Such approaches to communication are evident in the new breed of so-called 'knowledge management' systems being constructed by companies, where the organization's knowledge is stored in knowledge bases or knowledge repositories, accessible to all.

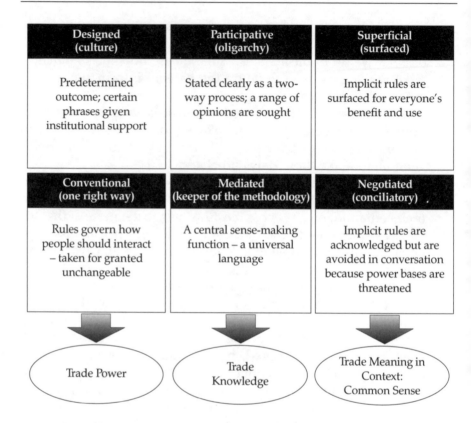

Figure 7.1   Communication grid

In some cases there are strict rules about who is allowed to construct a knowledge base (because left to their own devices, people tend to accumulate their own private knowledge bases), and strict definitions of what kind of knowledge is worthy of inclusion in the central archive. These rules are less strict in 'do and review', and people are encouraged to contribute to as well as to make use of the knowledge, but still within the leadership oligarchy's framework.

On the right of the grid, knowledge transcends the status of a mere commodity and becomes, in addition, the raw material of 'meaning in context' and 'common' sense. Although there are still rules for Activity Theory's 'actions' and 'operations', they are visible to all, and all can contribute to modifying or repealing them through 'activity'-level interaction. Sense-making is no longer confined to monarchs and oligarchs – it becomes a collective endeavour.

In 'gridlock', some of the 'rules of the meaning trade' remain sacrosanct and inhibit action, but in 'radically new', all rules are out in the open and negotiable. There are no high-level languages of organizational aspiration; just a desire to act on the common ground revealed by the trade in meaning.

Generally speaking, one can say that the rules of interaction become more visible, the voices involved become more numerous, and conversation has less to do with strategy and destination as one moves from left to right across the grid.

It is one thing, however, to acknowledge the value of 'acting on common ground', and quite another to know how to encourage the trade in meaning that is needed to reveal it.

The importance of dialogue

According to recent research into corporate restructuring by A.T. Kearney and leading European business school IMD (1997), much the most common method of achieving change is to replace the senior management team.

The survey showed that 75% of the top performers had changed management before restructuring, and only 32% of the rest of the sample of 211 responses had undergone such change.

We do not believe that this rite of management sacrifice (often at the behest of disenchanted shareholders) is the only or even the best way to achieve change. Our research has convinced us that the changeability of an organization, whether an integrated enterprise or partnership, has far more to do with its style of interaction and communication than with the competence or otherwise of its senior managers. Ritual management sacrifice only becomes necessary because other ways of 'unblocking' the organization's communication flows, and thus its ability to act, have either not worked or, more commonly, have not even been attempted.

We aim to show in this chapter how the 'radically new' approach to partnering has implications for communication conventions in all enterprises, not just partnerships. It is not painless, because it requires a new power structure, a new language and a new style of interaction that those with power to lose may find hard to accept.

They only have to do it from time to time, however, and if the alternative for vulnerable leaders of traditional, integrated organizations is to become ritual sacrifices on the altar of change, they may feel the communications programme we propose is worth considering. As for partnerships, we believe the techniques, principles and frameworks we will be discussing are vitally important if they genuinely wish to tap the full power of the Difference Engine.

In the usual monologue style of business conversation, senior managers use power (often unconsciously) to control meaning, belief or action. We are not suggesting they should surrender their power or abdicate their leadership responsibilities; we are suggesting they should be more conscious of the effect of their power, and should use it not to control and direct, but to create conditions for dialogue.

By 'dialogue' we mean communication that allows many voices and views to be heard. Only when there is a space for collective interpretation rather than persuasion can all the different views come together and produce some 'common' sense. Dialogue is made possible not just by individual dialogue skills, but by a conversation space, deliberately designed to encourage a different kind of talk that will lead to a different kind of action.

We are convinced that in this complex, fast-changing business world, where opportunities are fleeting and easily missed and emerging threats are obscure and unpredictable, the habits of dialogue, within integrated *and* partnership-based enterprises, can be an enormous competitive advantage.

Every conversation takes place within a context. The value of dialogue is that it makes the context an integral part of the conversation. It is an essential conversation for a 'radically new' partnership, because the only way to achieve the mutually satisfying outcomes partnerships seek is to hear what others are saying and sense what others are feeling before deciding what to do together.

From monologue to dialogue

A senior departmental manager with a UK-based multinational nuclear engineering company called a meeting of his staff to discuss 'empowering' them so that they would take 'continuous improvement' initiatives – at any rate, this was the official agenda for the meeting; the manager's real objective was to solicit views about what it was about their organization that did not seem to be working very well.

Participants were asked to say how 'satisfied' they were with the company, in relation to 11 characteristics of a 'learning company'. On the whole the meeting seemed to go well, although only the really confident staff members felt able to speak out in such a large group. There were a number of interesting discussions, including one about the usefulness or otherwise of the reward system. One member of staff felt that the reward system could be reviewed, and suggested some rather vague ideas about what could be done to improve it.

The departmental manager listened patiently to the criticisms of the existing system for a while, but when people started talking about their experience of different systems, he closed the conversation down decisively by listing the problems such change would cause, so preventing any further suggestions. In so doing, he was maintaining the conditions of a 'monologue', as opposed to a 'dialogue' which would have created the space for different views to be aired.

Dialogue has become a hot management topic recently, but much of the literature (see Dixon, 1996 for a good summary) elevates it to the status of an art-form. When dialogue is regarded as a pure, untainted, 'authentic' kind of conversation that can only occur between those initiated in its secrets, it becomes exclusive and thus of little practical use.

Sending people on courses to familiarize them with the habits and principles of dialogue can help, but it is the *outcome* of dialogue, not the process, that really matters. Conversations can never be wholly cleansed of power, prejudice and personal agendas. The important thing is that there should be a space for talk, in which they are part of the talk, not merely the hidden framework within which the talk takes place.

Our approach is both more modest and more ambitious than this: more modest because we see dialogue as an occasional event that does not require any special training, and more ambitious because we believe that everyone (or as many interested parties as possible) should be involved.

Dialogue obliges people to abide by certain rules that can be hard and even painful to follow, but the rules do not have to be learned by participants beforehand. They can be embedded in the structure of the conversation.

Five principles of dialogue

Rules are necessary in dialogue sessions, because dialogue is not a natural style of conversation for people used to the 'narrow-bandwidth' interaction typical in large organizations, where much, if not most, is left unsaid.

There are descriptions of a number of organized conversations with dialogue-fostering rules in Appendix C, but readers may wish to design their own. If they do, they should bear in mind the following principles, which all organized dialogue should abide by:

1   **Make it matter.** The agenda for organized dialogue must on no account be trivial. Dialogue can be painful, and people will be unwilling to endure the pain if the subject matter seems to them irrelevant or peripheral. Only issues of real substance should be addressed.
2   **Manage context, not content.** Provide an empty canvas. Let go of outcomes. The conversation must be allowed to manage itself.
3   **Keep things public.** Everyone must stay in the room, eavesdropping should be allowed, public records should never be

'edited', and corridor conversations should be conducted out loud.

4   **Let difference be seen and heard.** Keep the complexity. Let everyone tell their own stories. Don't minimize difference.

5   **Manage the language.** Make room for private conversation to be accessible, and encourage people to state the purpose of what they say when understanding becomes difficult. Outlaw jargon, and ensure the language is intelligible to everyone.

The Partnering Grid is a powerful dialogue tool because it reveals perceptions that might otherwise have remained hidden or implicit. By showing partners where all the perceptions of the partnership lie on the grid, misunderstandings will often become apparent, and explanations for puzzling behaviour will present themselves.

Although we have had many suggestions about how the labels we use on the Partnering Grid and its progeny could be improved, we have found that they, and their spatial relationships with each other, give people a 'script' and a place to start. They beg the kind of searching questions that reveal the tensions and contrasts that fuel the Difference Engine.

In this way, the Partnering Grid can be a useful platform for dialogue, by generating manifestly non-trivial topics for the sort of managed dialogues described in Appendix C to organize themselves around.

Electronic dialogue

All the techniques described in Appendix C can help promote a habit of dialogue in organizations used to monologue. They are all face-to-face, however. There is also a need to infuse other media with the new communications philosophy.

In the nascent science of human–computer interaction (HCI) it is possible to distinguish two very different approaches.

The first assumes that human beings and computers are 'information processors' that employ broadly similar mechanisms, and that a 'human–computer system' can therefore be constructed with a single set of methods and conceptual tools.

The second approach to HCI assumes that computers and human beings are different, and sees the objective of HCI as describing the wider context of human interaction with computers. Instead of assuming that human beings are equivalent to computers, it assumes that computers resemble human beings, in that both are involved in computer-using activities.

Activity Theory, discussed in Chapter 3, is a useful framework for the second approach. AT sees an IT network as a tool used in a social context. It is, or should be, designed as part of a larger interactive system that also includes richer media, such as face-to-face, to handle tasks with high levels of complexity or ambiguity. (See Box 7.1 for a classification of media according to their 'richness'.)

There is an art to matching the medium to the task, but there is a clear link in human–human interaction (and there should be in human–computer interaction) between 'medium-richness' and task complexity. It is 'inefficient' (wasteful of time or money) to use a richer than required medium, and 'ineffective' (it cannot do the job) to use a leaner medium than required. Human interactions should occur, and decisions should be made using a medium just rich enough for the purpose (see Figure 7.2).

It is often difficult to distinguish between AT's 'activity' and 'action', and 'action' and 'operation', but the idea that face-to-face meeting time should not be squandered on trivial 'operational' issues or that important 'activity' decisions should not be made with a mere exchange of faxes is hardly controversial.

AT provides a framework for making these trade-offs between efficiency and effectiveness, and it reveals the pressing need in partnerships for new, richer media that allow disparate and dispersed groups and individuals to engage in 'activity'-level tasks.

It has often been said that IT can help organizations change, but it cannot *lead* change. It can act as a powerful catalyst in developing a 'radically new' relationship, however, because the process of designing an appropriate IT network requires a prior discussion of interaction and decision-making that can reveal previously hidden rules and conventions.

Box 7.1 Measuring media-richness

Bob Lewis suggests that the richness of a particular medium can be expressed according to four parameters:

1 **Interactivity (speed of feedback).** Rich media provide an opportunity for immediate feedback, so participants may adjust messages 'in response to signals of understanding or misunderstanding, questions or interruptions' (Kraut et al., 1992, p.378). In this respect, synchronous media are richer than asynchronous media.

2 **Multiple cues.** Rich media employ a full range of verbal, paralinguistic, intonation, proxemic and kinetic cues (Lim and Benbasat, 1991) to convey intensity and subtlety of meaning, as well as literal content (Kraut et al., 1992). These 'surplus' cues are sometimes called 'social cues' (Daft et al., 1987; Farmer and Hyatt, 1994). Lean media employ a more limited range of cues. A face-to-face meeting is a rich medium in this respect, while text is lean.

3 **Language variety.** This is a measure of the range of meaning that language symbols convey (Farmer and Hyatt, 1994). Numbers convey more precision than natural language (Daft et al., 1987), while visual and graphic symbols carry a greater range of interpretations (Daft and Lengel, 1984). Higher-variety languages are more ambiguous, but can be used to organize larger amounts of information if there is a shared understanding of the language (Farmer and Hyatt, 1994). Rich media, such as video-conferencing, allow the use of high-variety languages; lean media, such as numeric databases, restrict language use to low-variety language.

4 **Social-emotional cues.** Cues related to 'social presence' have been somewhat neglected. Daft et al. (1987) define rich media as those in which 'personal feelings and emotions infuse the communication' and 'messages may be tailored to the frame of reference, needs and current situation of the receiver'.

A medium's potential richness can be thought of as the sum of the scores on each of these information-richness factors. In other words, 'richness' is defined by the medium's *potential* information-richness (potential, because actual richness is determined by how users perceive and use the medium).

By making the rules visible, IT makes them changeable, not by the technology itself, but by people who have been made aware of their weaknesses during the design process. As Lewis puts it: 'technology forces the folklore under the microscope'. An on-line meeting can involve any number of people. If it is to be used instead of face-to-face meetings, for instance, where the number of participants is constrained by room size and by who is on-site, questions arise about who should be invited.

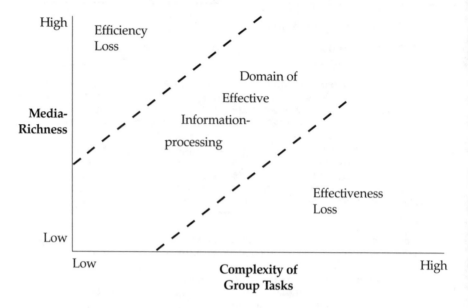

Figure 7.2   Communication choices

In organizations that live in a single building it is obvious that the knowledge of the organization belongs to all of its members. In distributed organizations, like partnerships, the collective ownership of knowledge is less self-evident. These tacit issues of ownership and access become explicit when an enterprise designs its electronic communications system.

The ease with which interactions through electronic media can be recorded make them catalytic in another way, too. As well as making interaction rules more visible, they can help build organizational memory. It is already common practice to store and distribute expertise and case histories on databases and through networks. In organizations where this memory-sharing is integrated with rather than merely an adjunct to face-to-face communication, the history of network traffic can become an incontrovertible 'log' of decision processes, assignments, undertakings and collective working practices that precludes the rewriting of history and helps to make the organization more improvable and more honest.

Moreover, the accumulation of such organizational memories in the records of the debates that led to the decisions can help the members of a community to understand each other better.

The underlying assumption in most discussions of the pros and cons of electronic and face-to-face communication is that the latter is the premium medium – the Concorde among the various available human interaction media. The implication is that if efficiency was not an issue, *all* communication would be face-to-face.

We take a different view. Face-to-face is the richest medium, and is essential for complex, equivocal tasks, but even if it were free (costless), it would not always be the first choice. There is much to be said for asynchronous communication, for example, because it gives communicators the chance to reflect on questions and issues before replying. Some people are more fluent and articulate when communicating electronically (when the power of others is less apparent) rather than face-to-face. For both these reasons, the creed of true dialogue is often better served by asynchronous and other electronic media than face-to-face encounters. Because the choices are there, we have to think about how we interact, and how we can make better (more efficient and effective) use of all available media.

Vast sums of money are being spent on IT systems designed to facilitate human interactions within distributed enterprises, but the opportunity to use system design processes to expose, corroborate and, if necessary, change existing conventions or implicit rules is usually missed.

IT has much more than new media to contribute to 'distributed enterprises' like partnerships. It offers a mirror to hold up against an organization's conventional patterns and styles of human interaction, and thus a chance to change things for the better.

Getting there

A partnership needs to develop a common language to help its members understand each other and their shared circumstances, because without a public, collective understanding, it cannot maximize the extent and scope of its common ground or exploit to the full its opportunity set.

We have argued that such a common language should incorporate two characteristics: the habits and rules of dialogue, and an integrated communications system which reflects rather than refracts natural human interaction. The media are, in a sense, the language. They provide its rich variety, and the judicious choice of a medium can ensure its efficient and effective use.

It should not be supposed that the rules of dialogue are only relevant in face-to-face communication. On the contrary, they should infuse the whole communications system, and are often easier to apply in non-face-to-face media. For example, rules of dialogue are embedded in the editorial policies applied on the letters page of the *JLP Gazette*, the house journal of the employee-owned UK retailer the John Lewis Partnership. Any member can write a letter to the editor anonymously; in so far as space allows, all letters are published, and if the letter is a request for information or a complaint, as many are, the manager concerned is obliged to respond to it there and then.

Similar rules of dialogue can be embedded in new media such as electronic forums and permanent conferences, where people are given space to vent their frustrations, point fingers and generally give voice to their fears or sense of injustice.

Sometimes these rules of openness are treated as a licence to be personally abusive or to launch subversive attacks on the organization's strategy or the conduct of its management. It is often tempting in such circumstances to break the rules by applying censorship, but that would merely reinforce older conventions that prevent dialogue.

Strict turn-taking, another important dialogue rule, can seem an unnatural constraint on the individual freedom so prized in Western culture. Some may rebel against the strictures, and 'dialogue tyrants' may be needed to enforce them, because there is always a temptation to regress to traditional styles of interaction.

The important point is that the pain and loss of face during the transition is quite natural. The new 'space' to which the rules of dialogue can take partnerships, or any other working communities, is more creative *because* it is more anxious. It is necessary to support people and help them deal with their anxiety, but the anxiety must never be designed out.

Our emphasis on dialogue in this chapter should not be construed as a claim that dialogue rules should govern all business conversations. As Figure 7.3 indicates, the challenge is to choose the most appropriate medium for the context, by which we mean the environment plus the objectives.

If the 'context' clearly points to the left of the grid, where power is centralized and fixed, the traditional conventions of communication are appropriate.

In the middle of the grid, where power remains centralized but knowledge is distributed and there is more participation, the kind of 'space' provided by quality circles, for example, is needed.

When the 'context' is on the right of the grid, where power and knowledge are both widely distributed, conventional styles of conversation are counter-productive because they prevent the expression of a multiplicity of views and the revelation of the complex collective purposes that are the inspirations of collaborative action. This is where new, rule-governed 'space' may be needed for conversation, and it is the 'leader's' job (see Chapter 8) to know when it is necessary, and make it available.

ARM's partnering style

Much of what we have said in this chapter about communication and human interaction is exemplified by the partnering style of the UK microprocessor intellectual property provider ARM described in Chapter 6.

ARM CEO Robin Saxby has two main axioms of partnering: 'Trust each other,' and 'Tell each other how it is.' The ARM credo is the opposite of the old 'knowledge is power' convention. 'We believe in communication,' Saxby insists. 'Our culture regards knowledge as useless, until it's shared.'

He admits that there are stresses in ARM's partnering arrangement: for example, ARM may have to compete with partners, can never recommend one partner to an end customer, and must

Context	Ethos	Learning Model	Use of IT	'Activity' Context	Information Richness	Complexity	Rule Transparency	IT Media
Implementing (habit)	What's right; one correct way	Teaching, coaching, modelling	Automating	Operation: unconscious	Lean	No uncertainty or ambiguity	Hidden	Calculation, data storage
Improving (asserting)	What works; norms maintained by gatekeepers	Critical review experiments	Informing	Action: individual, group	Mixed	Uncertainty (problems not puzzles)	Available but undiscussable	Info retrieval (text & numeric), e-mail
Integrating (mutuality)	Multiple views make up the whole	Collective interpretation; dialogue	Telemating	Activity: collective	Rich	Uncertainty, ambiguity	Negotiable	Computer-mediated communication conference and face-to-face

Figure 7.3 Effective use of communication media

be careful to avoid making decisions for customers. But Saxby says there have been few relationship problems.

One reason for this may be that ARM recognizes that, as Saxby puts it, 'there is no such thing as "a partner"'. He points out that ARM's partners and customers typically have several thousand employees (ARM had a little over 200 at the time of writing), and says that the partnerships consist not of formal agreements between companies, but of the 50 or more personal relationships between ARM staff and the people they deal with at partner and customer organizations.

'Trust has nothing to do with companies,' Saxby insists. 'It's between individuals. The people we deal with often trust us more than other employees of their own companies. You have to be discreet and fair; honesty is the best policy.'

ARM's partnering teams interact with people at all levels of its partner organizations, from the president downwards, and across all functions, from technical to marketing. 'Different parts of the team deal with different parts of the partner,' Saxby says. 'Our local people work with their local people. You have to deal in the partner's culture, not yours. We have people of 30 different nationalities at ARM, and a great deal of overseas operational experience.'

He regards ARM's poly-cultural nature as essential if the firm is to achieve its goal of having equal shares of its selected market segments in every region of the world. An additional advantage of ARM's broad cultural reach is that it means the company's eyes are always wide open and its ears are always close to the ground. It also means there are many different opinions about all sorts of things within the company, and Saxby regards that as an advantage, too.

Saxby values psychological as well as cultural difference, and thinks ARM has a good mixture of personality types. 'Some of our executives are paranoid, which means they're very good at checking for hidden bugs and preventing negative things from happening. Others are holistic and good at making positive things happen. We are against departments and for teams. We have found teams of marketing, engineering and finance people give the best results. Team leaders have to play their teams.

There have to be leaders – the challenge is to "grow" natural leaders. We need people who will do things.'

But the intimate personal relationships that are the stuff of durable business partnerships seldom develop spontaneously. You have to work at it. ARM is therefore pro-active in its partnering. It insists on regular partnership meetings, where 'silicon' and 'software' people, who in normal circumstances are reluctant even to acknowledge each other's existence, are obliged to interact face-to-face.

'We expose our engineers to the customers,' Saxby says. 'Every project team has customer members, and ARM staff are urged to step outside themselves and stand in their customers' shoes. Customers keep people honest. We also have a partnership task force. We shipped a bunch of people to the States, for a tour of partners. For some of the engineers, it was the highlight of their careers so far.'

According to Saxby, the foundation of a 'healthy' partnership is a 'shared outlook' (what we call 'common ground'). 'People will argue about anything,' he says. 'We have to find a common language and pictures and a set of terms all bound together by a common project plan. That requires flexibility, on both sides. If a new partner turns out to have very rigid rules of operating, the relationship is going to come unstuck. But it's during informal conversations, when you're having a meal together or in a car on the way to the airport, when you get real information. Our travel budget is horrendous, but it is the only way to get trust and real teamwork.'

He acknowledges, however, that things do not happen fast when you are working through partners. It can take three years to evaluate a partner, negotiate a contract, begin a project and get the product out, and that is a long time in high-technology. 'The challenge is to recognize that the world changes and to form a partnership that will last despite change,' Saxby says. 'You must let your partners make the contacts, because their customers want them not you, and you have to trust each other – we spend a lot of time working on that with group meetings and daily e-mail. And once you've done your last delivery, you must come up with a new reason for the partnership.'

In most ARM partnerships there are one or two key individuals in the customer organization that ARM calls 'disciples', with whom ARM has strong relationships. It can be very stressful when a disciple leaves, but a departing disciple is not a pure loss because he or she may, as disciples are wont to do, bring the ARM gospel to another company.

Ultimately, relationships between the individual members of a partnership will determine whether or not it works. There is little that leaders can do to force people to get on with and trust each other, but they can create the right climate and foster virtuous habits, such as the habit of dialogue.

Stories from the front

A painful brainstorm

In the summer of 1996, one of the authors went to Lausanne to speak at a conference about using information technology in research and development.

It became clear that all the participants – mostly academics, consultants or research managers – felt the R&D community had got carried away by IT, and that more face-to-face interaction was needed. The common view was that electronic communication had its place in R&D, but lacked the bandwidth (as the modern parlance has it) to handle the complexities the R&D community dealt in.

We were deep into our partnering research at the time, and it seemed appropriate to tell the conference something about the project and what we had learned so far. The presentation began with a warning that face-to-face interaction may be a solution, but it also posed a whole new set of problems.

To make the point, participants were divided into their three groups (academics, consultants, research managers), and asked to fill in the Partnering Grid and undertake what we call a 'complexity brainstorm' (see Appendix C) to look at how participants might work together after the conference.

A complexity brainstorm imposes rules of interaction designed to gather information prior to a search for answers. One participant (the organizer of the conference) repeatedly broke one of the rules by insisting on talking about what to do next during the initial information-gathering stage. The presenters said he was breaking the rules, and asked him to stop. He accepted the stricture, and complied.

It was a difficult moment, and made several participants feel uncomfortable. A week later, the presenters received an e-mail from a participant who was a mutual friend of theirs and the rule-breaker. He asked them whether they felt, looking back, they could have handled the situation another way that would not have caused the organizer to lose so much face.

The presenters thought about it long and hard, but concluded that they could not have saved the organizer's face without reinforcing the style of interaction the rules were designed to transcend. The question they had to answer, in the heat of the moment, was whether the organizer's face was more or less important than the rules. They decided it was less important, and that there could have been no collective gain without the individual pain that a major breach of the normal conventions of social discourse frequently causes.

Dialogue of the deaf

The Mondragón federation of industrial co-operatives in the Basque province in northern Spain is often held out as a model of how industry should be organized and how the spirit of common ownership and co-operation reconciles conflicting interests and promotes industrial harmony.

To understand the conflict that broke out at one of the federation's member companies in 1989, it is first necessary to understand the 'constitutional context': the distinctive system of corporate governance that prevails throughout the Mondragón federation.

To reflect their employee ownership, it is stipulated in the constitutions of all the members of the Mondragón federation that everyone has an equal vote in the *Asamblea General* ('General Assembly' – equivalent to the annual general meeting of shareholders).

The co-operative is governed on a day-to-day basis by three councils: a *Consejo Social* ('Social Council'), a consultative body that meets regularly and gives information and guidance to the *Consejo Rector* ('Governing Council' – equivalent to the non-executive tier of a two-tier board of directors), and the *Consejo de Director* ('Managing Council' – equivalent to the executive tier of a two-tier board, or the executive committee of a unitary board).

The members of the Social and Governing Councils are elected by the General Assembly, and members of the Managing Council are appointed by the Governing Council.

To many Western corporate governance experts, the system will doubtless appear unwieldy and not conducive to responsive or decisive management, but it has worked well over many years at Mondragón, and the potential for conflict between its constitutional components remained latent until an abrupt change occurred in the company's economic context towards the end of the 1980s.

Like most conventionally owned European manufacturers at that time, the company came under serious pressure from recession and intensifying competition, and by 1989 it was in imminent danger of collapse. The Governing Council responded to this crisis in an entirely conventional way, by appointing a new chief executive (CEO) with a brief to do whatever was needed to return the troubled company to profitability.

His prescriptions were conventional, too: he hired consultants and embarked on a rationalization programme that included substantial reductions in shop-floor and management staff, a de-layering of the hierarchy from six to three levels, and an attempt to induce everyone, not just the marketing people, to be more customer-focused.

The CEO was a strong and decisive leader. He had a clear idea of what had to be done, and he implemented the rescue plan in a firm if somewhat brusque way. Within three years, the firm was not only back from the brink but doing well again. It had all the hallmarks of a successful turn-round.

But the CEO's refusal to reflect the more onerous workload – the inevitable consequence of the downsizing and de-layering – in higher pay created a feeling of unease among the worker-members, and sowed the seeds of what would later become bitter disputes between the Social and Governing Councils.

In terms of the Partnering Grid, the CEO's rescue operation shifted the relationship between managers and worker-members from the original 'hearts and minds' to the 'arm's length' box, and many worker-members did not like it. Although the company was doing well again, it had lost its social cohesion, and the worker-members split into two camps: those who saw the CEO as a hero, and those who felt his decisive action had destroyed the precious spirit of co-operation that many who work within the Mondragón federation find so inspiring.

The social fragmentation was mirrored by disputes between the Social and Governing Councils, both of which, as noted above, are elected by the General Assembly. But although the debates between the two councils were vitally important, not only for the firm but also for the Mondragón federation as a whole, no real dialogue ensued. The Social Council kept criticizing the parlous state of labour relations, while the Governing Council contented itself with declarations of support for the CEO and the management. Positions became deeply entrenched, and the relationship became increasingly polarized.

The smouldering conflict ignited in 1993, when, in response to renewed competitive pressures, the CEO proposed an adjustment to the 'remuneration ratio' (the maximum multiple the highest salary can be of the lowest). Such ratios are vital symbols in producer co-operatives and 'alternative' management firms the world over, and people are always very sensitive about them.

Ben & Jerry's Homemade, a successful American ice-cream maker founded by Vietnam veterans Ben Cohen and Jerry Greenfield, is famous not only for such confections as Wavy Gravy, Chunky Monkey and Cherry Garcia, but also for holding annual general meetings in fields, giving 7.5% of profits to charity, buying ingredients from disadvantaged people and generally promoting the values and ethos of the responsible corporate citizen. From the start of the firm in 1977, Ben & Jerry's distinctive personality was also reflected in a rule limiting the highest salary to five times the lowest. In 1991, the reality of the market for senior executives obliged the firm to increase the ratio to 7:1, and in 1994, as Ben & Jerry's began looking for a new CEO to replace Ben Cohen, it removed all constraints on what it could pay its top managers.

In the Mondragón company's case, the maximum pay laid down in the company's constitution was 4.5 times the lowest wage. The CEO proposed, for exactly the same reasons that led Cohen and Greenfield to modify and then abandon their maximum, that the multiple be increased to 6.5:1, to reflect the extra pressure on managers in the more competitive climate.

Heated debates instantly erupted in the Social Council about the role of the CEO, what happens at other kinds of company, what it means to be a co-operative, and how much voice in such matters the worker-members should have. The managers insisted they had to have more discretion in the salary area, and that if their proposal was not approved, the company could go under in the highly competitive climate. The Social Council would have none of it, and called for a General Assembly.

The CEO spoke at the assembly, and said that the system could not work if his hands were tied. He argued that if everyone had to participate in everything, managers could not manage, claimed the firm's constitution was a democracy of delegates, not of direct representatives, and warned that how well people were paid depended ultimately on how well the firm performed.

This was like a red rag to a bull for the Social Council, and as one observer put it, 'a very strong, verbal confrontation' ensued.

The CEO reflected on his style, and adopted a softer line. He began coaching a successor, with whom he shared the leadership, and he tried to 'educate' members by sending them on courses to learn why the changes were necessary. He even put managers through a programme to improve their co-operative skills.

As the arguments about the pay ratio and the role of the CEO rumbled on, the company continued to do well, and before long the outside world recognized the CEO as an able leader. Early in 1996 he was promoted to the MCC (the governing Mondragón Co-operative Corporation), and was named 'businessman of the year' by a local employers' association.

The successor he had been grooming took over, and proved to be more disposed to dialogue. Relationships appeared to improve for a time, until, in an attempt to get the company closer to its customers, he proposed that holidays should be staggered from June to October, and that no one should take more than two weeks in August.

It may seem trivial, but as pay ratios are to co-operators, so August holidays are to Spaniards. Spain is shut in August. It was an incendiary proposal, and the worker-members rejected it out of hand.

The new CEO tried to win them over to his point of view with presentations and training programmes, and urged them to think in more businesslike ways, but although there were some good open discussions and an acceptance of the need for dialogue, neither side would budge on the holiday issue.

Positions became entrenched again. Both sides lost confidence in the other, and the mutual lack of trust made it impossible to promote the positive aspects of the relationship.

Everyone had a voice and everyone had their say, but although all knew they had to break the deadlock and understand the other side's position, the talk went round in circles. As one participant said, it was a 'dialogue of the deaf'.

The odd thing was that although the individuals on each side of the argument changed, the battle lines remained in exactly the same position and the language never altered. The company became unglued. Dialogue between managers and worker-members ceased, and the partnership, which began in 'hearts and minds', and which the previous CEO had tried to move to 'arm's length', ceased to exist.

Fortunately, the new CEO had a better feel for the tensions between business and community needs, and began to organize a different kind of conversation. Multi-stakeholder teams were convened, which began to discuss less controversial business issues in less confrontational ways, and as common ground was revealed, people slowly began to emerge from their entrenched positions.

In 1997, some people took holidays either side of August, and when others refused to budge, temporary worker-members were appointed, under special constitutional arrangements, to keep the firm going during the traditional holiday shut-down.

The new CEO has had some disagreements with his managers over the composition of the new project groups, but the company is still doing well, and as members continue to work together on business tasks, the wounds inflicted during the confrontation are gradually healing.

Summary

'Radically new' partnering requires a philosophy of communications based on collective sense-making, within rules of interaction accessible to all.

The rules of organized dialogue foster broader bandwidth interaction and reveal more possibilities for collaborative action.

Partnerships need to choose media with care, to ensure their communications are both efficient and effective.

Dialogue is not a panacea for all situations. It carries certain risks, and should be used with sensitivity to the partnership's context.

References

Blantern, C.J. (1997) 'The learning company: a strategy for sustainable development', in M. Pedlar, J. Burgoyne and T. Boydell (eds) *Dialogue and Organisational Learning* (2nd edn), McGraw-Hill, Chapter 22.

Daft, R.L. and Lengel, R.H. (1984) 'Information richness: a new approach to managerial behavior and organization design', *Research into Organizational Behavior*, 6.

Daft, R.L., Lengel, R.H. and Trevino, L. (1987) 'Message equivocality, media selection and manager performance: implications for information systems', *MIS Quarterly*, 11.

Dixon, N. (1996) *Perspectives on Dialogue*, Center for Creative Leadership.

Farmer, S.M. and Hyatt, C.W. (1994) 'Effects of task language demands and task complexity on computer-mediated work groups', *Small Group Research*, 25.

Kearney, A.T. (1997) 'Redefining the European restructuring agenda: a study of restructuring performance and future restructuring challenges', in *Redefining Restructuring: Toward Solid Growth*, A.T. Kearney.

Kraut, R., Galegher, J., Fish, R. and Chalfonte, B. (1992) 'Task requirements and media choice in collaborative writing', *Human–Computer Interaction*, 7.

Lim, F.J. and Benbasat, I. (1991) 'A communication-based framework for group interfaces in computer-supported collaboration', *Proceedings of the 24th Hawaiian Conference on System Sciences*, Los Almitos.

8 Somebody at the helm

Few aspects of management have attracted so much attention in recent years as the changing status and role of leadership.

According to a recent Lou Harris poll, barely 40% of American office workers believed the statement 'management is honest, upright and ethical' was 'very true'. In the European Union, the figure was 26%, and in Japan a mere 16% of office workers gave their managers the thumbs up (cited in Kouzes and Posner, 1993).

Other studies have revealed a similar lack of faith in the ability of their leaders to deliver long-term success among the employees of large businesses, and few people in the Western world hold their political leaders in such high regard today as they did even a decade ago.

Various explanations have been offered for the decline in the status of leaders and faith in them. Some say the 'globalization' of business is exposing the parochialism of leaders and their inability to grasp the implications of planetary management – that the modern global organization has, in accordance with the Peter Principle, outgrown the ability of one person or central team to lead it.

A modern variation on the same theme is that recent increases in rates of change and technological convergence have caused the required leadership reaction time to become so fast that traditional leaders no longer have enough time to gather and process the relevant information. Over the past 15 years, for example, the life-span of computer-based products has shrunk from four years to less than six months.

Others suggest that the decline in the stature of our leaders is the inevitable consequence of an increase in the intensity with which we scrutinize their performance; that it is not so much that our leaders have become less able to manage complex organizations, as the extent to which they are now being held personally responsible for the performance and the conduct of their firms.

James Meindl et al. (1985) have argued that we have a romantic idea of leadership which has caused us to attribute great potency to leaders, and to praise them extravagantly if they succeed and to damn them if they fail. We believe it is time to recognize that the age of romanticism is over, and we have to face up to the real causes of organizational success and failure.

It is not just employees and investors who pass judgment on the leaders of organizations. A host of environmental, social and regulatory groups, claiming to speak for an ever-growing constituency of 'stakeholders' and good causes, are pointing fingers at individual leaders and holding them accountable for all of the ills of the world, ranging from global warming and the reduction in bio-diversity to inner-city deprivation and rising long-term unemployment.

A parallel theme in the leadership debate is the notion that the role of leaders and leadership is changing – that the new circumstances demand a new 'paradigm' of leadership. The old idea of the leader as a general who plans, deploys and issues orders should be replaced, it is suggested, by new roles such as 'orchestrator', 'conductor', 'co-ordinator', 'ambassador', 'mentor' or 'coach'. If leaders or leadership teams cannot do what they used to do, it is argued, they must find a new role for themselves that addresses new needs.

Others suggest that the complexity of the modern environment makes the conventional 'solo' model of leadership less appropriate, because no one person can grasp all the implications of all the variables, and the future therefore belongs to leadership teams or systems. Some argue that the 'leadership pair' has long been the standard model in industries such as publishing (editor/publisher) and film-making (director/producer), and that this principle of divided leadership offers a way forward for many other industries and organizations.

The debate about whether chief executives should chair boards of directors, and the widespread view in Europe (although not in the USA) that they should not, is leading to the emergence of a 'separation of powers' principle in business, equivalent to the constitutional separation of legislative and executive power in a democracy. Separating governance from direction in this way creates a 'leadership pair' in business, consisting of the chairman and the chief executive.

But perhaps the clearest sign that something really important is at issue in the leadership debate is the paradox created by the idea of 'empowerment'. In its extreme form the paradox states that when leaders empower followers by requiring them to use their initiative and take responsibility for their own actions, they render leadership superfluous.

Empowerment is seen as desirable because it offers a solution to the problems traditional, centrally directed organizations encounter during times of rapid change, because of their lack of agility and adaptability. The conventional answer to the questions this begs about the role of leadership is that when leaders empower followers, they do so within the context of a residual leadership prerogative in the vital area of strategy formulation and direction-setting.

We believe this is a fudge, and that the questions empowerment raises about the role of leaders and the nature of leadership in modern organizations have yet to be answered. The fudge is nowhere more evident than in our 'radically new' partnerships, where the 'emergent' as opposed to 'intentional' nature of strategy (see Chapter 6) removes this alleged residual role of leadership in empowered organizations.

The paradox of leadership in the age of empowerment needs to be confronted head-on in partnerships. We need to know which, if any, of the traditional functions of leadership are still essential in distributed enterprises, composed of 'empowered' organizations and individuals. If strategy 'emerges' from the exploration of common ground, what service do leaders supply?

Leadership and the Partnering Grid

A common mistake of leaders is to overestimate the extent and potency of their authority. Sometimes they fail because they lack the ability to 'envision' and implement effectively, but often their shortcoming is a failure to understand the situation or the 'context' (environment plus objectives). They want things to be 'controllable', and they behave as if they believe they can make them controllable by an act of will.

If change programmes are not working, it is often a sign that someone somewhere has not done his or her homework on how others perceive the context. Sure, one can try to command and control directly, or dominate through 'culture', but ignoring other voices does not make them go away; it just causes change strategies to fail. Leaders need to understand the context if they are not to waste time, money and emotional commitment on change programmes that have no chance of success.

To begin our investigation of leading, leaders and leadership in partnerships, we will return to the Partnering Grid to see how its 'leadership' variant can help to fit leadership style to partnership context (see Figure 8.1).

The language of the grid makes it easy and, we believe, quite appropriate to think of leadership in the six boxes as having different characteristic activities.

On the left-hand side of the grid, the leadership – whether it be an individual, a pair or a group – 'dominates' in 'Command and Control', and 'integrates' in 'Hearts and Minds'. As we have seen, these two boxes are appropriate when both knowledge and power are concentrated. In both cases, leaderships can and do abrogate to themselves the right to manage both the ends and the means; they set the partnership's direction, and they also control, either directly through the power invested in them or indirectly through the homogeneous 'cultures' they design and impose, the implementation.

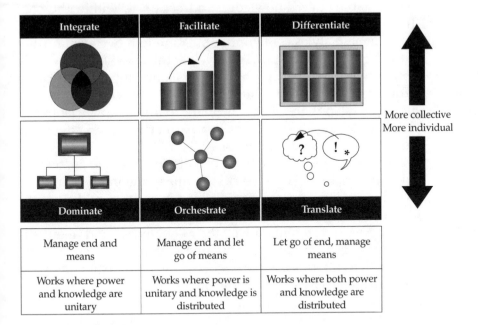

More collective
More individual

Figure 8.1   Leadership grid

When we move to the middle of the grid, the partnership power remains concentrated in the hands of a leadership oligarchy, but knowledge becomes more widely distributed, and it becomes impossible to dominate or to integrate. In 'Arm's Length', where difference is tolerated but partnership ambition is modest, the characteristic leadership activity is 'orchestration'. In 'Do and Review', where ambition is greater, the emphasis is on 'facilitation'. In both cases, the lack of a central 'brain', or control system, obliges leaders to relinquish their power to control the means, and content themselves with controlling the ends.

The distinction between 'orchestration' and 'facilitation' is subtle but important. It reflects differences in how the wide distribution of knowledge is perceived. In 'Arm's Length' it is seen as a regrettable fact of life that obviously requires a less 'hands-on' approach to management. In 'Do and Review', on the other hand, the wide distribution of knowledge is seen as a competitive challenge that can only be met effectively when people are free to gather new knowledge and act on it, within the constraints of the overall strategy.

Leadership styles come under pressure to move even further to the right, when the power as well as the knowledge is widely distributed, for in partnerships of this kind, any attempt by an individual partner to facilitate or orchestrate within an overall strategy will put the survival of the partnership in jeopardy. There is nothing so dangerous in a partnership as an attempt to wield a power you do not possess.

The characteristic leadership activity in 'Gridlock' is 'translation': leaders feel obliged to spend much time interpreting and trying to understand, to ensure all are in agreement, before the partnership acts. In 'Radically New', on the other hand, the partners are more sanguine about their differences and about the communications problems associated with them. They not only believe that difference is the engine of the partnership, they also revel in and celebrate it, and the only understanding they feel a need for is the understanding they need to act together.

One would have thought that as the context moves to the right of the grid, leaders or leadership teams should progressively relinquish power over the means in the middle column of the grid, and over the means *and* the ends in the right-hand column of the grid. This is a perfectly sensible way of looking at the grid, and contains more than an element of truth. However, we believe that when power and knowledge are widely distributed, a new role emerges for leadership which might be described as managing the process of collective sense-making.

We will devote the rest of this chapter to exploring this idea and its implications for leadership in partnering, starting with a discussion of a context on the threshold of 'Radically New'.

The case of the scientific research team

The academic research team is a useful laboratory for a study of leadership because it consists of able, highly motivated individuals trading in pure knowledge. It is a microcosm and, in many ways, the prototype of the knowledge-based partnerships that many management writers predict will become the dominant business life-form in the 21st century. We have integrated insights from this context with those emanating from the Partnering Grid to understand the direction leadership must take to perform effectively in this new environment.

In her unpublished doctoral thesis, Rose Trevelyan (1996) describes the leadership styles at various academic scientific research groups. One group, Team A, was led by George, who had an excellent track-record in his discipline but had stopped doing his own research ten years previously. He saw his role as securing funding for the team and acting as a 'control node' for communications within the team, and between the team and its external environment. Team members spoke to each other through him, but because his 'office' was some distance from where the researchers worked, the team as a whole was not very communicative, and when they did talk, they usually argued.

George reacted to events, and his team lacked a rhythm of work apart from the rhythm provided by the funding cycle.

Another research group, Team B, was led by Alice, who was also a first-rate scientist, but unlike George was still very involved in her own research. She spent a great deal of the time working at her bench alongside her colleagues, who both admired and respected her. She was not a very charismatic leader, but her colleagues recognized her talents, valued her experience and heeded her advice.

She had no particular view of her own role in the team, but when asked, her colleagues would say that she was a source of knowledge about 'the business of science' – about how to 'do' science, and how to succeed as a scientist – and had 'great contacts'. The team members were highly motivated, and seemed very satisfied with the team environment. The atmosphere was friendly and stimulating, and there was a great deal of talk about practically everything.

Alice gave the research a rhythm by instituting a series of meetings at which a member gave a presentation which was then discussed. This was good practice, because presenting ideas and research to peers is something ambitious scientists have to do more frequently as they become established. Alice assigned the presentation tasks, but she did not lead the discussions – she was just another member of the team.

The meetings and the collaboration they inspired helped the individual scientists by providing different perspectives on their work and exposing their assumptions to challenges from peers. The different backgrounds or hinterlands of members (from many different areas of chemical engineering) were made available to all, and the meetings were places to explore the differences and use them in each other's research. Constant communication and a convention of collaboration (helping each other with experiments, techniques and interpretations) also helped to make good use of the differences.

One of the things Team B members say is that they feel 'there is somebody at the helm'. They do not mean by this that there is a captain on the bridge who has a clear idea of where the ship should be going; they mean that there is someone who can be relied upon to get funding, point out the shoals and rocks that lie ahead, warn people in time for them to take evasive action, and generally encourage the research directions most likely to be successful.

There is no real overall direction in academic research. You have to 'conjecture boldly', and then follow where your tests or experiments lead. A strong, specific sense of direction is actually quite dangerous in science, because it can constrain the imagination and lead a researcher to ignore the oddities and inconsistencies that often lead to new knowledge.

However, there is a great deal to be said for establishing a clear framework for research and having someone around who is familiar with the rules and conventions that must be followed if good science is to be recognized as such by the scientific establishment. Young scientists need role models and mentors to show them the ropes and help them to get connected to the relevant networks. They need to be able to talk to people who are streetwise in the business of science – who know the best journals to be published in and the criteria editors use when selecting papers, what conferences or seminars they should go to, whom they should speak to or consult with, and what prizes to enter for.

Research scientists do not need leaders; they need counsellors and confidant(e)s. They do not need someone to tell them what to do or where to go in their research; they need someone to tell them when they are going wrong, veering off track, or not making the right contacts and connections.

In short, they need people who know the rules of the game and how to question them, who know what to do when the colleagues question the rules, and who are always available because they are always there. Team B had all that, and it showed in their results.

The best measure of a scientific research group's performance is its publishing success, measured by an index of the number of articles published each year, weighted by the 'visibility' of the journals (visibility is the best available proxy for quality). The Institute of Scientific Information publishes a *Science Citation Index* which ranks journals according to how often they are cited, and awards them a Journal Impact Factor that relates the total number of references in all journals in subsequent years to the articles in the journal in any one year.

To measure the performance of research groups, Trevelyan used an index based on the number of articles the group published in each journal, multiplied by the journal's Impact Factor. The score for Team A was 2.7, the average for all the groups she studied was 4.2, and the score for Team B was 4.9.

She also used a measure of job satisfaction (from Hackman and Oldham's *Job Diagnostic Survey*) as an outcome variable. The average for the members of Team A was 5.2 (out of a maximum of 7), the average for all the groups studied was 5.3, and the average for Team B was 6.

The context of scientific research teams exemplifies the kind of context the leaders of modern knowledge-based businesses find themselves in, and it is no accident that many such companies strive hard to cultivate a collegiate, academic atmosphere in their workspace.

We need to go beyond this model, however, because in contexts where 'Radically New' is the only appropriate box, power cannot be embodied in an individual like a team leader. Our model of leadership must accommodate partnership situations in which all rules and rulers can be challenged, and where no one is in control.

The new leadership

Trevelyan's work on scientific research teams illuminates the style of leadership needed within the modern knowledge-based organization. Combining her insights with those gleaned from the Partnering Grid and our partnering research produces the following provisional list of new leadership guidelines:

- Use signals, not directions, and focus more on *who* people are, rather than on *where* they are or should be going.
- Accept, reveal, validate and then celebrate differences by seeking them out and making them part of the common ground (as Alice tried to do). There was much more communication within Alice's team. Differences were 'processed' through information-sharing and group discussions.
- Take nothing for granted. Challenge assumptions, question motives (including your own), and get the inevitable battles for power and influence out in the open (as George failed to do). At Alice's meetings, assumptions were always being challenged, and motives were frequently questioned.
- Be there, because by being there you can help to legitimize both individual and group action. Alice spent a great deal of time in the lab. She was available to other members of her group, and her silence was as eloquent as her occasional interventions.
- Let go. Trust people, because only the trusted can become trustworthy.
- Recognize that since groups get their energy and direction from the ambitions of their members, leaders have to follow where their followers lead. Traditional 'strong' leadership (based on confirming and controlling one unique reality) is a weakness when reality is in the eye of the beholder.

This list of guidelines is provisional because it begs more questions than it answers. It advocates a renunciation of the traditional leadership roles without providing specifications for a new role.

Reading between the lines of the six guidelines, however, one can just discern the shadow of a shape that encompasses but does not control, that supports but does not direct, and that proscribes but does not prescribe. It is a negative kind of leadership, which prevents those led from falling over cliffs (like J.D. Salinger's *Catcher in the Rye*), but is otherwise content to facilitate and act as a passive role model.

If the context permits the source of such leadership to be an individual or a group of senior partners, this description is consistent with the 'do and review' characterization of leaders as facilitators. The same preventive kind of leadership is needed when power is too widely distributed for an individual or small group to supply it.

Perhaps the best way to describe it is that in 'radically new' partnerships and other loosely linked enterprises, the role of leadership is to construct and maintain a 'soft container' within which each of the led is free to pursue his or her own life-plan and thereby help to generate the group's 'emergent' strategy. No easy task, one might think, and it is made doubly difficult by the requirement in 'radically new' that this 'soft container' be constructed and maintained collectively, not by an individual or group.

Leading by containing

The role of leadership is to create space for different kinds of interaction, and to be extremely sensitive to the nuances of context. Nowadays, there are more voices and more competing realities than ever before, and in partnerships where power and knowledge are both widely distributed and must therefore be constantly traded, there is no escaping them.

A way is needed of making 'common' sense of the cacophony by discovering what everyone thinks and feels, and it cannot be supplied by the traditional idea of leadership as embodied in an individual, if the context does not permit it.

Like Sartre's hell, context is other people, and it cannot be understood unless everyone has a chance to express his or her views and reveal his or her aims, assumptions and prejudices. Context as 'other people' delineates the common ground and acts as the frame of collective action.

The frame of action that it is the leadership's job to divine and maintain consists not of the mechanical cause-and-effect levers managers are taught to identify and manipulate, but of a general ambience within which creative collective action is encouraged. In W.P. Kinsella's story *Shoeless Joe* (on which the film *Field of Dreams* was based), the protagonist is told: 'If you build it, they will come.' That is the leadership's job: to build it, and wait for them to come.

As we have seen, the leaders of today's complex organizations must accept that in modern environments they cannot realize long-term plans. They can, however, guide their enterprises, teams or organizations into a creative space by tuning the various elements that contribute to the ambience.

These elements include such qualities as the level of anxiety (as we have seen, too little anxiety is as bad as too much), the distribution of power and knowledge, and what we call 'the philosophy of communications'.

As one moves across the grid, power and knowledge become more widely distributed and are transmuted from levers to aspects of relationships. But there are limits to the extent to which power can be allowed to dissipate. In 'radically new' there is no central power, but when there is no power of any kind, the partnership degenerates into chaos. In 'radically new', power is widely distributed, but a vestige of leadership remains in the form of a collective, self-managing system that contains anxiety while allowing people to challenge and subvert it.

This begs questions about the nature of 'good enough, but not too good' containment, and of control systems that provide 'a little bit more than not enough' security. We plan to conduct more research here, but the notion of leadership as a disembodied 'container' is a useful starting point that allows us to expand our provisional list of leadership guidelines.

Systems that say 'no'

An axiom in the philosophy of science is that although it is impossible to prove a theory is true, it *is* possible to prove a theory is false. According to this view, scientific advance is driven not by the verification of new theories, but by the falsification of old theories, and the way to strengthen or corroborate a theory is to think of experiments that could disprove it.

It is the same with 'radically new' leadership. The way to help people is not to tell them what to do, but to create a system that will tell them when they seem to be barking up the wrong tree, reinventing the wheel or heading down roads others have proved to be dead ends.

Accompanying this guardian role is a responsibility to handle the consequences of advising people to stop: to pour salve on bruised egos, for instance, to explain why it is advisable to stop, to describe the implications of not stopping, and to do all this without discouraging your protégé, from exploring new avenues and continuing to take risks.

People, particularly those able, self-confident professionals on whom most enterprises rely, do not like being told that they are wasting their time. They much prefer to be patted on the back and urged to get on with it. The 'stop' signal must be used sparingly, therefore, and when issuing it, the system's credentials for doing so must not only be in plain view; they must also be debatable.

People will not heed the advice to stop or to change course unless they believe those giving the advice are qualified to do so, and they will not learn from being stopped unless they have the opportunity to question or challenge the advice, and to negotiate the terms and timing of subsequent uses of the 'stop' signal. Perhaps most important of all, they are unlikely to heed a leadership system that will not heed them when they tell it to stop.

Being the rules

The credentials of leaders to issue 'stop' signals consist not so much of their experience, wisdom and power of patronage as their knowledge of the 'rules', and the relative breadth and richness of their networks.

Alice was seen to be qualified to stop people because she was seen to be streetwise in the ways of science. Her canniness and intimacy with the strange goings-on within the scientific establishment were seen by her colleagues as a valuable team resource – a vicarious sensing system that extended their own knowledge of right and wrong and good and bad.

Every goal-seeking group operates within sets of rules. There are social rules that govern interaction within groups, rules of etiquette that govern interaction between groups, and meta-rules associated with occupations and professions that govern the behaviour of individuals and how they conduct themselves in relationships. The rules of interaction can be implicit and fixed (left-grid), mutable (mid-grid) or explicit (right-grid). Few of these rules are 'lawlike', in the sense that they can be clearly articulated; most take the form of conventions governing social interaction, and are thus highly context-specific.

The rules are embedded in a good leadership system, but they are not written down and stuck up on notice-boards. They are part of the context, and are only invoked when necessary. When people know the leadership system has their interests at heart, the mere absence of red lights will contain anxiety and sustain momentum.

In time, they will absorb the rules of their game and become qualified to be members of the leadership system themselves, but until then they need to know that rules they have yet to encounter exist, and that there is somebody, or some system, at the helm to stop them and help them explore the implications of breaking the rules.

Good leaders dislike rules because they know they reduce the degrees of freedom, but they will not hesitate to apply those that should not be transgressed. From time to time they may impose and police temporary rules, such as the dialogue rules of a complexity brainstorm (see Appendix C), to make a point, or reveal problems and opportunities that have been hidden or obscured. They may also suspend rules temporarily, by controlling turn-taking in group meetings, for example, or by preventing people from changing the subject when they become uncomfortable or impatient.

Rules channel and focus rather than constrain, and it is the job of leaders and leadership systems to know them, to show how they fit together, to apply them, to explain them and to *be* them. They do this in scientific research groups, for example, when they insist on experimental controls and urge researchers to read and cite other people's work.

Managing paradox

However well endowed with rules and conventions, and however well led, individuals and teams are always encountering inconsistency, conflict, ambiguity and paradox.

There is the conflict between the interests of the individual and the interests of the collective, for example. The respect we feel for our leaders does not prevent us from challenging them. We yearn for security in an increasingly unstable world, and our desire for certainty grows as we are besieged by its opposite on all sides.

All this equivocation and conflict creates anxiety, a certain amount of which is both appropriate and healthy. But there is a limit to how much anxiety people can handle. Anxiety can be stimulating in small doses, but can be quite incapacitating in large doses. It needs to be 'contained', and the paradoxes and inconsistencies that cause it must be resolved or otherwise alleviated.

This containment of anxiety is also part of leadership's role in working communities, poised on the creative brink of total instability. The leader, or leadership system, must appear to be used to and unfazed by all the uncertainty, and leaders and members of the leadership system can help people acquire the same tolerance, not by removing it, but by confronting it and coming to terms with it.

They can help people appreciate the limits of rationality and the constructive aspects of conflict. They can say that it is OK to be different, that paradox is where the action is, and that it is quite possible for two apparently conflicting views to be equally true. They can translate, interpret, summarize, categorize and show how the apparently conflicting interests of the individual and the collective are reconciled in common ground.

Above all, they can give the members of their group a sense of their and the group's place in all the confused uncertainty, and provide answers to existential questions such as 'What is the point?'

Rewards and feedback

The vast majority of people who join organizations and groups to pursue their own ambitions in collective endeavours do so with great enthusiasm and high expectations. In other words, they start off highly motivated. It is one of the tasks of a leadership system to ensure that the initial fiat of enthusiasm is sustained by the containment provided by the group.

An academic research team exemplifies this challenge, because research scientists are highly motivated individuals who see research projects as stepping-stones. They want to be members of successful research teams, because the team's success will enhance their own reputations and take them a step nearer to achieving their own goals, such as winning a Nobel Prize, for example, or leading their own research teams.

What they require of a leader, therefore, and what will deter them from leaving to join another research team, are guidance and feedback on their progress towards their personal goals and personal recognition. They must be paid enough to contain their material anxiety, of course, but they also want credit where credit is due – they want their ideas and contributions to group success to be fully and publicly acknowledged by the inclusion of their names on published papers, for example, or mentions in public presentations of group research. The leader's role is vital here, because such attributions and acknowledgements are usually in his or her gift.

The desire for recognition, and the *right kind* of recognition, is very strong, and people need to be confident that it will be routinely given. They must trust their leaders not only to know what the right kind of recognition is, but to distribute it fairly and to explain the reasons for withholding it.

Faith in just rewards is part of the containment leaders and leadership systems provide for self-motivated individuals and groups. It is as necessary in a partnership as in an academic research team, because without it relationships will become strained and may eventually come apart.

What constitutes 'just rewards' depends on circumstances and the organization. Reward systems help to define cultures, and in partnerships, what individual members see as 'just reward' may vary enormously. It is vital, therefore, that everyone in the partnership should know what each of their partners wants and how their wants are changing, and it is the job of leaders or leadership systems to ensure everyone gets as much of what they want as possible.

Recognizing transitions

The social dynamics of a collective enterprise are constantly changing as the stages of projects or projects themselves are completed, and as people join, develop and move on. When new recruits join, they need a lot of guidance and support, but as their confidence grows, they become more self-sufficient and more familiar with the 'rules of the game'.

In partnerships, of course, the most important 'rule' is that the rules of the game are complex patchworks of sets of rules, and that members need to know to whom each set belongs, whose interests they serve, how they can be questioned, and who can do the questioning.

Leaders need to be aware of these subtle transitions, and to act accordingly. They must know when their erstwhile apprentices have become masters, and sometimes they may need to hand over leadership to others who have become better qualified or have a better sense of what the issues are in a particular area or project.

It has been said that one of the responsibilities of a leader is to make him or herself redundant. In enterprises such as partnerships where power is widely distributed, the baton of leadership, or membership of the leadership system, should be free to move as the leader of a flock of flying geese shifts when the wind veers or the avian navigation system demands a course correction.

Constant transitions from the role of patron or protector to the role of colleague or follower (and back again) show that the leadership system is working well; that people are growing; that pride, jealousy and the battles for power or to save face are not distorting or petrifying the group's containment.

When leadership is seen as being fluid rather than embodied, leaders are always asking themselves if they are the 'right' person to lead at this particular time, and given the skills, aptitudes and experience of team members, whether there is a need for any conventional leadership at all.

Leadership 'experts' often claim that although a talented group of musicians can make wonderful music without a score, no one has suggested that a symphony orchestra can operate without a conductor. Oh yes they have! Richard Hackman (1996) has studied the Orpheus Orchestra, which does very well without a leader or a conductor. He says that although there is often a lot of argument during rehearsals, the conflicts are always resolved before the performance begins.

There is some debate about whether the Orpheus needs some kind of 'business manager' to handle administration and the money side of things, such as negotiations with sponsors, recording companies and concert hall owners, but there appears to be no obvious reason why such functions could not be carried out by non-musicians, acting as hired administrators or agents.

Keeping it going

When strategy is 'emergent' and 'granular' (in the sense that it consists of a series of more or less discrete projects or tasks), the question arises: 'How does one persuade people to turn up after one project has been completed and the next has yet to begin?' What is it that maintains a group's integrity and energy when there is no long-term plan?

Leadership is part of the answer, because leaders can sustain the interest of members in the potential of the relationship by making space available for collective interpretations and the mutual exploration of hinterlands.

There will always be discontinuities in relationships – times when people pause for breath and reflect on whether they have gone as far as they can in this group towards achieving their personal goals, and whether it is therefore time to move on. In these circumstances, the group, if it is to survive, needs someone to persuade people that the best is yet to come. This is best done not by passionate appeals for unity or tirades against 'traitors' or by the painting of grand visions, but by establishing, through dialogue, whether the group's common ground has been fully explored, or whether more opportunities exist to prove the group is still worth more than the sum of its parts.

Relationships should be abandoned when they have ceased to be value-creating, but many are ended prematurely because their members have not taken the trouble to explore the full extent of the common ground. We believe that for most partnerships it is best to assume that common ground grows as it is acted upon, and that abandonment is almost always a mistake.

But if no one insists that the dialogue occurs, preferably at regular intervals, no one will know that the abandonment is a mistake until it is too late.

Making communication public

Successful groups are obsessive communicators. Members talk a lot with one another, are deeply interested in what is going on outside the group in areas of interest to them and their fellow members, and are constantly interacting and learning in their efforts to improve their understanding.

People do not have to be encouraged to be curious; they learn spontaneously, often unconsciously. It is part of a leader's task to ensure that the natural human hunger for knowledge is kept well fed, and that their knowledge is rendered useful by sharing it. Leaders and leadership systems cannot direct the learning, because they cannot know what is important. All they can do is cultivate a space where the habits of learning and open communication can flourish.

Neural networks learn automatically through a technique known as 'back propagation of errors'. When attempting to solve problems, for example, they guess initially, test their guess against reality, record the imperfections, and then send them back through the network to adjust 'connection weights' (the strength of connections between individual neurones).

If such artificial neural networks accurately reflect the way human brains learn, all that is needed for learning to occur spontaneously is a set of interesting problems and sufficient information to check the accuracy of each successive guess at the solution. Leaders can help to satisfy these requirements by making information available – in on-line databases and well-equipped libraries, for example – encouraging open, non-recriminatory discussion of errors, and doing all they can to increase the connectivity between network nodes.

Leaders should be gate-openers, as well as gatekeepers. They can 'facilitate' communications and the flow of information by providing appropriate 'means' (databases, meetings, access to experts, etc.) and, where appropriate, by taking charge of the group's (as opposed to the individual's) social interaction.

Rose Trevelyan observes that when left to their own devices, scientists can get so preoccupied with their work that they switch off socially, and become incommunicado. Their intense focus is necessary, but it should be interrupted from time to time by regular meetings and the cultivation of the habit of socializing. 'Scientists have to be encouraged to be a group,' Trevelyan says, 'because their basic attitude is that they are on their own.' Alice, leader of the more successful academic research group, maintained a strict meeting schedule, and did what she could to cultivate a communicative atmosphere.

From leaders to leadership systems

Our thesis in this chapter is that leadership in the modern distributed organization is not about directing, inspiring or motivating, but about providing suitable 'containment' in the form of rules, conventions, parameters and support systems.

A Future Search Event (see Appendix C) is a container in this sense: it is a shell of dialogue rules within which partners can discover more about what already unites them. To convene such an event and to persuade others to attend is an act of leadership.

The containment is 'soft', in the sense that it can be pushed into new shapes by those contained, but 'strong' in the sense that it is in no one's interests to breach it.

The leadership system provides and maintains containment, but has no power within the space contained. The system's members are bound, like everyone else, by the containment, and have no special power over internal content and processes as long as the latter are consistent with rules and conventions embedded in the containment. It can play a part in the self-management, but cannot control it. Its role is to provide a space where people feel secure (but not too secure), and to equip it with the tools, sensors and support partners need to understand each other and decide what to do together.

We shall conclude this chapter by summarizing how the styles of leadership, and their psychological consequences on those led, change as different contexts require movement across the grid from left to right.

In the 'Command and Control' and 'Hearts and Minds' boxes, where difference is seen as dysfunctional and thus to be minimized, leaders are involved in almost everything, from 'envisioning' and selling plans and strategies to controlling the minutiae of content and processes. They have no need to design systems of containment because everything is already under their own control.

Individuals feel secure, but imprisoned.

In 'Arm's Length' and 'Do and Review', where difference is seen as inevitable and is tolerated, a crude but still rigid kind of containment makes an appearance. Because difference has to be lived with, leaders are obliged to relinquish some of their control over content, but they retain control over processes. They are the keepers of all methodologies, and although they do more facilitating than their counterparts on the left side of the grid, they still orchestrate and direct. Outcomes are not planned in great detail, but leaders still control them indirectly, through their power to manipulate processes.

Individuals feel less secure, but more liberated.

In the 'Gridlock' and 'Radically New' boxes, where difference is not only tolerated but is seen as the motive power of the group or partnership, leaders relinquish their control over content *and* processes. This makes people feel free, but insecure and anxious. Some containment is still necessary, therefore, to keep anxiety within bounds and legitimize difference, but it is a 'softer', more flexible containment than that provided in the mid-grid by the leadership's control over processes.

It takes the form of a set of general behavioural (as opposed to specific process) rules, such as rules that say that scientists innovate and publish, artists create and exhibit, accountants analyse and report, as well as rules of dialogue, designed to reveal common ground and permit the precious shared resource of difference to be fully exploited.

The containment also consists of rule-policing activity by a leadership system (through signals rather than instructions), which encourages the trial-and-error learning characteristic of neural networks. People are left to their own devices, and are only made aware of the rules when they appear to be about to break them. Security comes not from instructions, but from knowing that everything that is not proscribed is legitimate.

The presence of a minimal but good enough containment of this kind will lead to a high level of creativity, and the gradual emergence of mutual trust and a shared sense of destiny.

Story from the front: HHCL

This case study is derived from a Marketing Council/London Business School joint initiative on a range of issues relating to innovation.

Howell Henry Chaldecott Lury and Partners is an innovative British marketing and communications agency responsible for a number of high-impact campaigns, some of which have tested the boundaries of the acceptable in advertising. Clients love them.

The partners attribute their success to the unusual nature of their working relationships, inside and outside the firm, and the way in which the organization of work groups reflects the firm's core values.

The groups are multi-functional, and 'client-focused', in the sense that each group works on a separate client account. The common goal for all group members is to generate 'competitive advantage' for clients. Campaigns are 'owned' by all members of the group, and everyone contributes at each stage. Clients are often present at group meetings – their involvement makes them 'part of the problem-solving, not part of the problem'.

Like any organization, they aim to build trust within working groups, but they seek trust in an unconventional way based on an assumption about why people are there. They assume that each person wishes to succeed. This frees them from suspicion, and allows collaboration instead of negotiation. Trust is easily achieved, but this is only the start. Initially, ideas within everyone's comfort zones are tabled, but the real creativity occurs when ideas beyond the comfort zone begin to flow. When everyone's 'on board' and while keeping in mind the objective of producing high-impact campaigns, basic assumptions about how the client communicates with its stakeholders begin to be challenged.

At the start of the process there is no known outcome. Nobody leads anybody anywhere. Solidarity within the group is based on the desire to provide the best service for the client, the wish to do something different within the profession, and the knowledge that everybody wants and intends to collaborate.

'Howell Henry is held together by the never ending journey of constantly creating competitive advantage,' said co-founder Adam Lury.

The most important measure of performance and source of pride for Howell Henry people is increases in client sales. Winning awards for creativity (a frequent occurrence for the firm) is not an important driver. Howell Henry people are externally focused (towards the client), not internally focused (towards their peers).

The firm does not have 'departments'; it recruits people with particular functional expertise. Teams are composed of people with these different backgrounds, such as account planners, media strategists, creatives and financial experts. The absence of conventional departments requires 'experts' to talk most with people from other areas of expertise, rather than with colleagues. This reduces the use of jargon and professional language, and the tribalism that often leads to conflict which traditional organizations often have to deal with.

Every member of an account team is involved at every stage of the project. This transforms the traditional, linear process of campaign creation, where the final product is passed from one department to another, into a truly collaborative effort. Creative ideas often come from media strategists, and a media strategy often comes from an account planner. All members are experts in their own fields, but they do not stick to their own fields.

Clients are involved throughout the process, because they see the ideas before they get to the final stage. The group says to the client: 'You know where we are in this process. This isn't a meeting about selling you the new work, or presenting anything to you. We're just saying this is what we've done in the last two weeks and we'd like your feelings about it.'

Howell Henry people find these meetings very liberating. They say there's such a variety of knowledge, expertise and energy in the room, and such a high value is placed on novelty, that creative ideas for campaigns are almost inevitable.

Summary

Leadership styles must fit organizational needs and contexts.

The scientific research team poses an interesting challenge for leaders, and provides insight into what the knowledge- and partnership-based organization of the 21st century might look like. It suggests that leaders' role is to provide a framework rather than a direction.

In 'radically new' partnerships, where, like the research team, power and knowledge are widely distributed, leaders are replaced by leadership systems.

References

Hackman, R. (1996) 'An unusual organisation: an orchestra with no conductor and shifting roles', paper presented at the Academy of Management Annual Conference, Cincinnati.

Kouzes, J. and Posner, B. (1993) *Credibility: How Leaders Gain it and Lose it, Why People Demand it*, Jossey-Bass.

Meindl, J., Ehrlich, S. and Dukerich, J. (1985) 'The romance of leadership', *Administrative Science Quarterly*, vol.30.

Trevelyan, R. (1996) 'Leadership and Work Attitudes in Academic Biochemical Research Groups', unpublished doctoral thesis, University of London.

9 On trust and conflict

According to Francis Fukuyama (1995), the social virtues and the 'art of association' vary from culture to culture, and 'high-trust' societies, such as Germany and Japan, are better at creating large organizations that do not rely for their integrity on family ties and state ownership than 'low-trust' societies, such as France and China.

In recent years, some management writers have also identified trust as a crucial ingredient in the building and maintenance of large organizations (for example, Whitney, 1993; Block, 1993).

If, as all these writers claim, trust (or 'social capital', as Fukuyama also calls it) is the 'glue' that binds associations of people together without the help of kinship ties or state ownership, no book about partnering would be complete without a discussion of its origins and significance.

Most recent work on partnering has assigned a central role to trust and the avoidance of conflict. We do not. According to the model of partnering presented here, trust is not a prime mover, precondition or *sine qua non*, but just a consequence of acting together, within contexts. And as contexts vary, so the quality of trust that develops within them varies.

In this final chapter, we shall see what light the Partnering Grid can shed on the role of trust in all organizations, not just partnerships, and discuss the very different perspective it offers on the problem of conflict before concluding with a brief list of the major principles that have guided us in the writing of this book.

Dimensions of trust

It is important to distinguish between different varieties of trust, because Fukuyama would have us believe that there is only one kind of trust, and that only those fortunate enough to have grown up in 'high-trust' societies will be capable of forming durable partnerships with each other.

In the age of global markets, one cannot accept this cultural limitation on partnering. We need to look at trust not as an aspect of national culture – as a quality that exists in some places and not in others – but as something that emerges as a result of collective action, and moreover, as something that can take various forms.

The Partnering Grid provides such a perspective.

Figure 9.1 shows that the degree of trust rises as a partnership becomes more ambitious, but that the quality of trust needed to sustain ambitious partnerships varies as one moves across the grid.

The trust that moves partnerships from 'command and control' to 'hearts and minds' is a trust born of sameness and consensus. People trust each other because they share a common culture and understand the behaviour that it demands of its members. Therefore, the way to promote this kind of trust, and thus to move up the grid, is to choose similar partners and develop a strong, shared culture.

The trust that moves partnerships from 'arm's length' to 'do and review' is a trust born of experience and the development of mutual respect. People learn to trust each other by working together, and as each project is successfully completed, trust

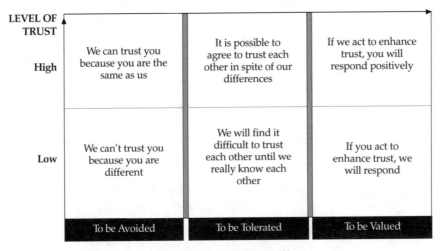

How Partners View Difference

Figure 9.1   Perspectives on trust

grows. The way to promote this kind of trust is to foster the belief in both or all parties that the relationship(s) will be long-term, and that each project, in addition to being value-creating in its own right, is an opportunity for the partners to learn how to work better together.

The trust that moves partnerships from 'gridlock' to 'radically new' is a trust born of the recognition of mutual interest. People trust each other because they see no reason not to. They are aware of all the risks, but have concluded there is too much to be gained by both or all the partners for it to be in the interests of any of them to reward trust with betrayal. The way to promote this kind of trust is for the partners to be open with each other about their strengths and weaknesses and their hopes and fears, at ease with the differences between them, and so obviously committed to the relationship that it is inconceivable that any partner would place their individual interests above those of the partnership.

Trust, in other words, is related to *perceived risk*. It exists in 'hearts and minds' because risk is low, it grows in 'do and review' because risk reduces, and it is endemic in 'radically new' because the perceptions of the risks in relationships are over-whelmed by the perceptions of the likely rewards.

The way a partner responds to questions about trust and risk can often be illuminating. In one case, three partners answered a set of questions about trust, and the results were used to plot their positions on the Partnering Grid. They were all in the 'Value Difference' column, but two were close together at the top, and the other was less than halfway up.

It transpired that the reason for the vertical difference was that the third partner in 'Gridlock' perceived a type of risk in the rela-tionship that was not applicable to the others and had not occurred to them. The revelation of the difference in the percep-tions of risk intrigued all three partners, and was accordingly dis-cussed at some length.

Following the discussion, the isolated partner said: 'Now that you understand how I see my own particular risks, I'm not so worried about them.' The diagnosis itself, and the discussion that followed, had brought about an upward movement to a more trusting relationship.

Trust is a substitute for control. It is an automatic kind of indi-vidual self-control that emerges, unbidden, from joint actions that lead to mutually beneficial outcomes.

The case against partnering

The story of the Mondragón federation member company at the end of Chapter 7 will strike a chord among company leaders who have experimented with partnering and decided that it is not for them.

The case against partnering is that although the strategy of bringing together two or more complementary sets of skills or resources without anyone paying for them seems attractive in theory, the theory takes no account of the often incompatible cul-tural baggage also brought together in such unions.

The sceptics may readily admit that the technical and process linking required in partnering can be accomplished relatively easily and harmoniously, as long as the interfacing occurs at the right levels, and they may even acknowledge that skills can also be connected without much difficulty, as long as the right people are doing the connecting.

'But that's the easy part,' they will argue:

The real problem is that this linking of processes and skills will only create the value promised by the theory if individuals from quite different cultures can learn to work well together, if not on day one, at least within a few months.

Speed is of the essence nowadays, and companies simply can't afford the months and years it sometimes takes to bed-down a partnership, still less spare the management resources needed to resolve the rows that will always break out when no one is in control.

Those who advocate partnering should try it. It is extremely difficult to manage two contrasting cultures. They are always rubbing each other up the wrong way, and without the authority that comes with ownership, the conflict soon gets out of hand and destroys any chance of capturing the synergy.

It's like when an American spacecraft docks with a Russian one. The docking mechanism works OK, and the two craft become physically one, but once the crews have embraced, the show is over. They can't do useful work together because they can't understand a word the other crew are saying. And even if they could communicate verbally, their cultural differences would prevent all but the most trivial collaboration.

There is no conflict between American and Russian astronauts after a space docking, because no attempts have to be made to bridge the cultural abyss that divides them. If a joint work programme is to be undertaken, however, cultures as well as spacecraft would have to dock, and the chances are the process would generate conflict, if not between the crews, at least between the mission control teams planning the work.

As events on the *Mir* space station in 1997 showed, crisis can act as a powerful catalyst in cultural docking. In this case, impending catastrophe brought the 'active' cultural interface up from the ground into *Mir*, and perfect cultural docking was quickly achieved in the shared language of engineering.

It is true that the personal conflict on which many promising business partnerships founder is mostly caused by a rubbing together of the 'soft' cultural baggage that accompanies the 'hard' technical, process and skills inputs of the partners. But there is no getting away from it: whether one likes it or not, that is in the nature of partnerships. Skills, however technically compatible, cannot be docked to create the joint capability the partners seek without an effective docking of the partners' respective cultures.

There is nothing wrong with the analysis of the sceptics. The mistakes they make are in the conclusions they draw from it.

The first is the tacit assumption that cultural conflict is a problem peculiar to partnerships, and that when one company acquires another, it soon absorbs the latter's culture. This is clearly not so. Cultural tribalism can be just as violent between acquirer and acquired as it can be between partners, and because money has been paid, it can be much more costly.

The second, more serious mistake is to assume that conflict is a barrier to effective docking, and that the only associations between companies that create value are those in which all is sweetness and light, within a peace imposed by *force majeure*.

Aspects of conflict

According to the conventional view, conflict is dysfunctional because it distracts attention from management's proper external concerns, wastes resources on resolving conflict, and can put the integrity of the whole enterprise – be it a company or partnership – at risk.

Richard Pascale (1990) challenges this view, and argues that conflict is a creative force that endows organizations that tolerate and foster it with more creativity and flexibility than their consensus-seeking rivals.

There is too much evidence to support both these views for it to be reasonable to reject either. Conflict plainly can lead to, or at least is plainly not inconsistent with, creativity and flexibility, and it can clearly become pathological and lead to the termination of working relationships.

The trouble with the obvious resolution to this dilemma – that one should foster enough conflict to generate creativity, but not so much that stability is jeopardized – is that it is hard to judge beforehand the point at which conflict stops being a virtue and becomes a vice. When those persuaded by Pascale's thesis begin to vie with each other to see who can crank up conflict levers the furthest, they have no way of knowing, before it is too late, how far they can go.

Our research has convinced us that this debate about conflict is based on a false premise. Conflict is not, as many assume, an independent, unmanageable variable in the calculus of co-operation that occurs spontaneously whenever cultures meet. It is, rather, a symptom of attempts to minimize or otherwise manage the differences between partners.

When one begins to see conflict as a docking procedure – as a language or protocol for achieving optimum interface between significantly different partners – the question, 'What is the right dosage of conflict?' is replaced by the question, 'How different can two prospective partners be from each other and still achieve a mutually satisfactory docking?'

Richard Pascale says the trick is 'to disagree, without being disagreeable'. We have argued in this book that the trick is 'to be different, without being incompatible'.

The Difference Engine

Our research has convinced us that difference, whether or not it is manifested in conflict, is an essential ingredient of the new kind of strategically ambitious partnering now being adopted, because without difference there can be no synergy and no positive sum to the partnering game.

Conflict is often no more than a testing procedure – a way to compare, explore and understand the merits or otherwise of different ideas, approaches, attitudes and values. Too many partnerships are abandoned because the behaviour they inspire is perceived as conflict, and therefore destructive and to be avoided, when the same behaviour could just as plausibly have been perceived as argument, debate or dialogue, and therefore constructive and to be welcomed.

One of the great virtues of partnering is that if differences are not so great that the union collapses, the partners can learn as much about themselves as they do about each other. People who have their own ideas, approaches, attitudes and values but respect yours are people you can do business with.

It is difference, therefore, not conflict which is the engine of creativity. Conflict is a symptom of intimacy, a sign that partners have cut through their superficial similarities and started to tap the power of the Difference Engine.

Whether it is perceived as conflict, argument or debate, such docking or alignment behaviour is an essential part of the mutual exploration of cultures and attitudes. It can get out of hand, of course, but as long as the partners are compatible and have a positive-sum game to play together, it need not.

In ambitious partnerships, an absence of conflict should be a cause for greater concern than its presence, for it suggests a lack of the mutual exploration that is the prerequisite of creative partnerships.

But not all partnerships have high ambitions, and the degrees of conflict it is worth enduring and trying to manage depend ultimately on the context, the objectives of the partners, and the environment. There are as many reasons for partnering as there are partnerships, and it would be fruitless to struggle with difference if all one wanted to do with a partner was to prepare the ground for a divestment or present a united front to a regulator or a potential competitor.

The trouble is that the current state of the partnering art provides no guidance on what partnership qualities are best suited to particular partnership objectives. Partners may be clear about what their objectives are, and yet unsure about what kind of relationship they need and how much conflict to encourage or tolerate when trying to achieve them.

It is too hit and miss. Before partnering becomes a reliable solution to the very wide range of business problems that it is theoretically applicable to, it must cease to be a black art and a lottery, and become, if not a science, at least an art of a whiter hue, that people can talk about sensibly, and by talking about it, learn to understand it.

Partnering 'lore'

It was because we saw the need for a 'language' of partnering to illuminate and help develop the partnering art that we undertook the collaborative research on the results of which this book is largely based.

We believe in partnering and in the power of the positive-sum game, and we wanted to get a firmer conceptual grip than has hitherto been achieved on the slippery, subtle, multi-faceted complexities of the personal relationships, perceptions and misconceptions of which they consist and on which the success or failure of a partnership depends.

One thing we have found is that although there is no lore of partnering, there is no shortage of conflicting assumptions, convictions and beliefs about the idea. There are passionate evangelists and equally passionate sceptics; there are those who see partnering as fundamental and strategic and those who see it as little more than a label with which to embellish relationships with suppliers. There are those who advocate intimacy and those who prescribe arm's length relationships; those who believe in sharing everything with their partners and those who jealously protect what they see as their 'core competences', on the grounds that within every partner there lurks a potential competitor.

Our research suggests that although these disagreements about what partnerships are or should be and what they might or might not become profoundly influence how those involved in partnerships behave, many are misconceptions, and others are not really disagreements at all, but become, when looked at from a different angle, equally logical and often compatible ways of looking at the same relationship.

We hope we have helped to provide this 'different angle', and that those who believe in the power of the Difference Engine in partnerships – and within their own organizations, too – will have learned something useful from this book.

Epilogue

While writing this book we accumulated a set of beliefs and rules of thumb that we kept quoting at each other. We felt it might be useful to conclude with them.

They fall into two groups: general, and partnering-specific.

General principles

- There are no uniquely valid truths. Other people's stories are real.
- 'Knowledge' is a matter of personal opinion.
- If you want to change, change the way you see difference.
- Dialogue means action, not just talk.
- You can never get all the cards on the table.
- Keep turning the kaleidoscope.

Partnering principles

- Partnerships consist of nothing but the perceptions of their partners.
- Make space for the common ground to be seen.
- Look for 'fit', not solutions.
- Seek difference, not deference.
- Looking at difference differently can build trust.
- Harmony is not creative.
- Context is everything.
- Power is always moving and being redistributed.
- Strategy is not intended, it 'emerges'.

These principles do not fit well with the conventional wisdom and philosophy of management, but it is our belief that those who heed them, and who embrace the main prescriptions of this book, will establish for themselves a competitive edge in the new era of partnership enterprise.

Summary

Trust is widely seen as a necessary precondition for success in partnering, and conflict is widely seen as a sign of impending failure.

This book sees trust as a consequence of acting together on common ground, despite differences, and conflict as a consequence of attempts to minimize differences.

Partnerships will only realize the full power of the Difference Engine when they accept that trust and conflict are aspects of the way difference is viewed and managed.

References

Block, P. (1993) *Stewardship*, Berett-Koehler.
Fukuyama, F. (1995) *Trust: The Social Virtues and the Creation of Prosperity*, The Free Press.
Pascale, R. (1990) *Managing on the Edge: How Successful Companies use Conflict to Stay Ahead*, Simon & Schuster.
Whitney, J.O. (1993) *The Trust Factor*, McGraw-Hill.

Appendix A: Partnering Grid self-test

To give readers a feel for what it is like to work with the Partnering Grid, we invite them to complete the following questionnaire. The diagnostic we developed as a result of our research is based upon priorities, preferences and relative weightings. This means that rather than giving an absolute position from which to draw universal conclusions, it is used to enable partners to compare and discuss the different ways the partnership presents itself to them with a view to unravelling tacit assumptions and building a richer picture for effective collaboration.

The calculations involved for the full version of the grid do not lend themselves to pen and paper, so we have used a much simpler approach here which, although not statistically valid, captures the feel and spirit of a conversational diagnostic – one that gives 'food for talk'.

Each of the six sets of statements below refers to one of the boxes on the grid. By scoring the statements and adding up your total score for each set, you will get a picture of the relative weighting you currently place on the different approaches to partnering.

It is unlikely that a person or organization will display the characteristics of only one style. In practice each of the boxes on the Partnering Grid always consists of elements from all the other boxes. Hence the diagnostic points to a current dominant preference, not to an absolute position.

A box which presents itself as dominant when considering one task may be virtually non-existent in the context of another task. We change our positions on the grid in response to actions, and even within a single conversation. It is therefore important to have a specific task in mind when answering the questions, and not to focus in a general way on the relationship itself.

We are no better qualified to interpret your results than you are. Indeed, the results themselves mean little without some idea of what they mean for the individual concerned. For this reason, we suggest you get at least one other person to complete the questionnaire around a single task so that meaning can be extracted from the differences that emerge.

Questionnaire

Think of a critical work or business task in your partnering context, and tick the box which best represents how you currently view this task:

		Strongly disagree	Disagree	Neutral	Agree	Strongly agree
1	Our organizational cultures are strongly aligned.	☐	☐	☐	☐	☐
2	We enter a partnership with a strong shared vision.	☐	☐	☐	☐	☐
3	We meet regularly to address emerging needs.	☐	☐	☐	☐	☐
4	We focus on clear communications.	☐	☐	☐	☐	☐
5	Knowledge is widely distributed across the partnership.	☐	☐	☐	☐	☐
6	The more we pre-plan things, the better.	☐	☐	☐	☐	☐
7	We develop new ways of working at the interface.	☐	☐	☐	☐	☐
8	We are concerned about conflicting objectives.	☐	☐	☐	☐	☐

9	We look for a common language for understanding.	☐	☐	☐	☐	☐
10	We make sure our values are clear from the outset.	☐	☐	☐	☐	☐
11	A small management group makes the major decisions.	☐	☐	☐	☐	☐
12	We acknowledge multiple purposes.	☐	☐	☐	☐	☐
13	We focus on learning and continuous improvement.	☐	☐	☐	☐	☐
14	We compromise to maintain political stability.	☐	☐	☐	☐	☐
15	We establish common standards of behaviour in advance.	☐	☐	☐	☐	☐
16	We establish protocols for dealing with our differences.	☐	☐	☐	☐	☐
17	It is often difficult to be understood.	☐	☐	☐	☐	☐
18	Many different views of the partnership are necessary.	☐	☐	☐	☐	☐
19	Some differences have to be planned for.	☐	☐	☐	☐	☐
20	We work at maintaining harmony.	☐	☐	☐	☐	☐
21	We encourage participation in decision-making processes.	☐	☐	☐	☐	☐
22	It is necessary to satisfy many stakeholders before things can get done.	☐	☐	☐	☐	☐
23	We establish clear rules and structures.	☐	☐	☐	☐	☐
24	Power to get things done is in the hands of many stakeholders.	☐	☐	☐	☐	☐

To score your questionnaire give scores for each statement as follows:

Strongly disagree	**Disagree**	**Neutral**	**Agree**	**Strongly agree**
1	**2**	**3**	**4**	**5**

Calculate your score for each set of statements using the following key:

Hearts and Minds	=	☐ 1	☐ 2	☐ 10	☐ 20
Command and Control	=	☐ 6	☐ 11	☐ 15	☐ 23
Do and Review	=	☐ 3	☐ 7	☐ 13	☐ 21
Arm's Length	=	☐ 4	☐ 9	☐ 16	☐ 19
Radically New	=	☐ 5	☐ 12	☐ 18	☐ 24
Gridlock	=	☐ 8	☐ 14	☐ 17	☐ 22

Enter your total scores in the appropriate box on the grid below:

Hearts and Minds	Do and Review	Radically New
☐	☐	☐
Command and Control	Arm's Length	Gridlock
☐	☐	☐

Compare your results with a partner's score on the same task, and formulate the five most important questions that each of you now wants to ask the other.

Appendix B: Ways of knowing

Contrasting modern and postmodern logic

The terms 'modernism' and 'postmodernism' refer to two different systems of belief for making sense of things. The difference between them is most easily understood when their conclusions are compared, because postmodernism is not a coherent theory, but rather a growing set of related theories and outlooks associated with a wide range of disciplines, all of which, in their different ways, challenge the modernist, scientific paradigm which has dominated the Western world of thought since the Enlightenment.

Our purpose in offering this brief glimpse of two contrasting ways of making sense of things is to help promote a general recognition that the growing fragmentation and diversity of the world we live in requires new ways of thinking about that world, and about our place in it.

To demonstrate the contrast between the two outlooks, we have compared modern and postmodern perspectives about a number of issues that are central to partnering, and we have posed a set of partnering-related questions begged by the post-modernist perspective.

We hope the questions and your answers to them may serve as a starting point when developing new ways of working together.

Control

Modern

We are in control – we can predict the future with sufficient accuracy to allow us to plan and be reasonably confident that outcomes will be more or less 'as planned'. Because we are in control, we can co-ordinate and create order.

Postmodern

Being in control is a story we tell to validate a scientific way of seeing the world, but many other stories are available to us that can give shape and direction to our lives. When we abandon the quest for control, we enable ourselves to look at connection and collaboration.

Truth

Modern

The world is knowable and concrete, and a discovered truth can be applied universally. We are constantly learning more about the fundamental laws that govern the physical world.

Postmodern

The more we search for truth, the less 'knowable' and the more abstract the world becomes. Even the fundamental particles of matter exist in many forms which are affected by the mere act of observation. There is no single truth about anything which is valid in all circumstances, and at all times.

Self

Modern

We have an inner self which is the source of our knowing and our direction. Individuals are the agents of change – thought precedes action.

Postmodern

All knowledge, including what we know about ourselves, is the creation of social processes, mediated by language – language precedes thought.

Ideology

Modern

All action begins with ideas which are right or wrong, better or worse. There is one right way to see the world, and we are unable to act until we understand.

Postmodern

Action emerges from shared meaning in a particular community. Understanding is context-specific, and comes from doing things together. There are many valid ways of seeing the world.

Progress

Modern

We are creating a better society through our understanding of moral good and our mastery of the physical world.

Postmodern

We are working together amidst the paradoxes of our lives and purposes to do the best we can for ourselves and each other.

Language and reality

Modern

Language is a transparent window, through which we can convey messages about a reality which, notwithstanding a thin veneer of cultural nuance, is more or less the same for everyone. It is, in other words, a relatively pure medium of communication and representation.

Postmodern

Language represents, and also constitutes, realities which are not concrete or objectively knowable. The truth is not 'out there' – it depends on how we see and talk about it. Language or meaning can never be pure because we can never separate them from our purposes in our relationships with others.

Some questions to help frame our partnerships

- How do we proceed when our differences of view and opinion reflect not differences in perceptions of reality, but different realities altogether?
- How can we make room for people to speak for themselves, and how do we ensure that what they say is accepted as true for them?
- How can we open our eyes to the possibility that things are not as we see them, and learn to focus on our relationships and collective tasks rather than our local solutions?
- How do we ensure that when we play down control, what takes its place is not just hierarchy by another name?
- How can we work together effectively when consensus is an agreement that is always being negotiated?
- How can we learn more effectively and autonomously and then act without first insisting that we all understand the world in exactly the same way?

- How do we construct 'systems' for managing or directing our enterprises when we have learned to see them as consisting not of individuals, but of relationships?
- How should we perceive leadership in a world where unitary meaning and purpose are unlikely to be of lasting value?

Suggested reading

Crawford, M. (1995) *Talking Difference: On Gender and Language*, Sage Publications.

Fairclough, N. (1989) *Language and Power*, Longman.

Gergen, K. (1996) *Saturated Self*, Basic Books.

Morgan, G. (1997) *Images of Organization*, Sage Publications.

Rorty, R. (1989) *Contingency, Irony and Solidarity*, Cambridge University Press.

Appendix C: Tools for dialogue

The approach to dialogue described in Chapter 7 focused not only on the ability of individuals to convey what they mean, but also on the conventions and conversational architectures that determine what we can say to each other and therefore do together. This appendix briefly describes a number of models of managed conversation that can bring the hidden contexts of talk into plain view, and thereby both increase the depth and extend the scope of individual and collective efforts.

We are all competent communicators already, so we do not need an elaborate set of new skills to engage in dialogue. Indeed, attempts to acquire such a 'skill set' could actually inhibit dialogue by reducing the differences that make dialogue such a revealing form of talk. The prerequisites of dialogue are not individual dialogue skills but conversational frameworks that enable people to speak and hear across the boundaries of their differences without having to learn a new language.

The frameworks described below intervene in the mechanisms of communication to increase our chances of making common sense.

Future Search

A 'Future Search' is a three-day 'multi-stakeholder planning event', designed to reveal co-operative potential by finding out what the participants are already willing and able to do together. Its designers, Weisbord and Janoff, were inspired by the US community involvement 'futures conferences' organized by Eva Shindler-Rainman and Ron Lippitt in the 1970s, and the 'search process' used at the Bristol Siddeley Aircraft Engine Co. in England in 1960 by Eric Trist and Fred Emery (Weisbord et al., 1992).

A Future Search does not seek to persuade participants of the merits of a specific vision or goal. It has the more modest objective of uncovering what Weisbord and Janoff call 'common ground'.

Hundreds of Future Searches have been run in the USA, in the public, private and non-profitmaking sectors, addressing issues ranging from strategic design to planning the economic future of communities. Firms that have held Future Searches include AT&T, Digital, Nissan and the publishers Jossey-Bass.

As we have noted, large organizations, including partnerships, are complex systems that cannot be 'known' in their entirety, but a Future Search attended by a sufficiently large number of representatives from a sufficiently large number of the system's subsystems can reveal the system's general 'shape' and those open spaces where there is enough agreement to act.

It consists of four basic components:

1 Building a shared personal, local and global picture of the past that shows participants that they live in the same world and share a lot, despite their differences.
2 Mind-mapping the present, focusing on trends like the trend towards partnering, for example, geographical developments, housing and racial issues or equality of opportunity, and asking what the trends reflect. People then split up into their own stakeholder groups and draw their own mind maps.
3 All the stakeholder groups then report back with brief two-minute presentations on their 'Prouds' and 'Sorries' – the

things they are most proud of, and the things they most regret.

4 Participants are then reorganized into mixed groups again, and given two-and-a-half hours to imagine an ideal future and identify the obstacles that have to be overcome if it is to be achieved. This is what Weisbord and Janoff call a 'reality dialogue'. The aim is to establish what people are ready, willing and able to do already, without compulsion or compromise.

Typically, participants are astonished by the correspondences between their individual views, particularly of the past and the future. They have been so focused on the differences and disagreements between them in the present that they have had little inkling of how similarly they see what has gone before and where they should be going.

This realization that there is more that unites than divides them can reveal the possibility for a new kind of 'strategy' that is not handed down from the top, but rather emerges from relationships and agreements. Strategy loses its grandeur and privilege, and becomes a derivative of relationships. And, by the same token, the role of leaders ceases to be the devising of strategy and becomes the cultivation of the conditions for strategy to work.

In Chapter 7 we saw how this suspension of difference and focus on common ground can be maintained after the event with the help of the Partnering Grid and rules for dialogue, for it is all too easy after a horizon-expanding event like a Future Search for participants to relapse on returning to work into the same old conflict relationships.

Open Space Technology

The objective of Harrison Owen's Open Space Conference is to create a space where what he calls 'breakthrough ideas' can emerge. The design of the meeting reflects Owen's belief that the really productive parts of conferences are not the formal sessions, but the breaks in between them (Owen, 1992).

The meeting is held in a large, sparsely furnished room with a lot of wall space on which to post ideas and notices.

A typical conference lasts for two or three days, and is run according to Owen's rules:

- There is a theme, but no agenda.
- No one is in charge.
- Whoever is there are the right people.
- When it's over, it's over.
- The meeting starts with everyone sitting in a circle.
- People choose issues on which to sponsor group discussions.
- Participants sign up for the groups that interest them.
- Sponsors convene groups, lead discussions and take notes.
- The notes are fed into computers and made available to all.
- New topics are identified for discussion each day.
- 'The rule of two feet' requires people to leave the group or meeting if they are not learning or contributing.

Owen says that this lack of form allows ideas to assume their own shape, undistorted by status or politics. The structure is designed to allow people to say the things they really feel strongly about, unfettered by the conventions imposed by what the organization expects of them, in their current roles, and so find new connections and new possibilities for action.

Real-time Strategic Change

Like Future Search and Open Space, Real-time Strategic Change is a 'whole-system-in-the-room' event (the 'real-time' refers to simultaneous planning and implementation). The objective is to address current organizational issues in terms of their connections with the whole system (Jacobs, 1994).

As many people as possible from as many constituencies and stakeholder groups as possible (external as well as internal) are invited to ensure:

- a data-rich, complex, composite picture of 'organizational reality'
- that shared insights form the basis of subsequent partnerships that would previously have been inconceivable
- that all key stakeholders understand, accept and can use the broad, whole-picture views when deciding if, when and how to do business in the future.

Real-time Strategic Change can involve up to 2 000 people in three-day meetings. Facilitators set task and time limits, but the discussions within the whole group and the sub-groups are not structured, and there is an emphasis on truth-telling and honesty.

This event requires the leadership to play a more active role than in other such interventions. The meeting usually begins with a welcome by the leadership to demonstrate its power to shape strategy, time is set aside for the leadership to reply to questions, and the leadership is responsible for deriving a strategy from the information generated.

Action-learning

This process was developed by Reginald Revans fifty years ago in the English coalfields. Originally designed to help colliery managers solve difficult production problems, it has two goals:

- to solve long-standing problems
- to enable people to learn with and from others by discussing difficulties each member of the 'learning set' encounters while working on the problem (Revans, 1980).

A typical action-learning programme begins with a large-group workshop lasting three to five days, followed by a prolonged period of small-group work on specific problems at weekly or bi-weekly meetings over a period of six to nine months. Work design is left to the set itself, aided by a set adviser, or a 'comrade in adversity' as Revans calls the role.

The nature of the problems addressed is critical – they must be important to the organization, complex and not amenable to conventional approaches or solutions. In a conventional task, group learning is incidental. In action-learning, it is one of the objectives.

Assumptions are challenged, and the results of actions have to be confronted. Because sets are responsible for implementing as well as planning, much of the learning comes from trying to persuade others to help solve implementation problems.

The system is based on four adult-learning principles:

- Managers learn best from each other.
- Managers learn from reflecting on how they are addressing real problems.
- Managers learn when they can question assumptions on which their actions are based.
- Managers learn when they receive accurate feedback from others and the results of their problem-solving actions.

It embraces two organizational principles:

- Issues are soluble by people who care about them.
- Members who have no previous involvement with the issue can offer fresh ideas that can lead to innovative solutions.

Interpreting Partnering Grid data

In our partnering work, we often ask a broad cross-section of stakeholders in the partnership to complete a software-based diagnostic which plots an individual grid position and shows the different ways in which such positions can be arrived at. We do not interpret the data for them: we give the groups the data to interpret for themselves. The groups are shown how to manage the programme, and are then left to interpret the data in whatever way seems to make the most sense to them.

We usually ask them to use the data to formulate the two most important questions they would like to ask each of the other groups, thus making the discussion a conversation, and giving more people a chance to partake in the sense-making process. Two rules are rigidly applied to assist the process:

- people can only ask questions to which they do not know the answers
- responses must always relate directly with the questions, not to other responses.

The complexity brainstorm

The complexity brainstorm is another example of a 'regulated dialogue'. It is a group activity, designed to derive a much richer picture of the 'situation' than would be possible with conventional methods of interaction. Its main distinguishing characteristic is that it seeks a group rather than an individual view.

A group consisting of a representative cross-section of the partnership gathers round a large expanse of paper (roll ends of newsprint are ideal), and the theme of their task or meeting is placed in a circle at the centre. Participants are asked to shout out anything that comes into their heads that seems to them to reflect current reality in the partnership.

The comments can be about anything from market conditions and global affairs to personal observations on current internal issues. The one stipulation is that they must be descriptive, not prescriptive. This rule restrains people from offering pet solutions – the objective is to build up a complex picture of the current situation. The comments are written down as they are uttered, in a neutral colour.

In most brainstorms, the next step is for the group to try to make 'collective sense' of all these individual observations. The usual method is to reach an agreement about reality and priorities for action. The problem with this approach is that people discuss what they see in relation to what they think will happen and what each wants to achieve, so the discussion often degenerates into wrangles about whose view should count most before decisions are made. The group never gets a chance to discover what people really mean, or to confront the task of finding enough in common to work together despite the fact that they see things differently.

In this case, rules are introduced to outlaw the traditional sub-texts of such sessions: battles of will, power or influence. Participants are asked to indicate the significant issues by ringing them and showing how they link together, but they are asked to do this not according to their own or their sub-group's interests, but on behalf of the whole group. They are asked: 'If the group had a voice, what would it say?'

Most people quickly realize that they lack the data to comply with the request, because they do not know enough about what others feel and perceive. They are given a chance to satisfy their curiosity by asking questions (one each for a large group, two each for a smaller group) designed to elicit the information they need to complete their task. This constraint on questioning slows the conversation down and obliges people to listen carefully to each other and to themselves.

The questions and answers often reveal hidden assumptions and personal beliefs that are sometimes surprising and invariably illuminating.

When the question allocations are used up, each 'stakeholder' group is asked to say what seems to them to be significant to the whole group, and responses are ringed in each group's chosen colour. The groups are not allowed to talk about this in private; they must negotiate their sub-group view in front of the whole group. The purpose is to bring conversations which are usually private into a public space, so that everyone has more data to go on.

The completed map thus consists of a set of diagrams (circles linked by lines), each in a distinctive sub-group colour, and each representing what the sub-group assumes the whole group thinks. Some diagrams overlap, but no two are identical. What sub-groups see in similar ways is clear, but differences are also clearly apparent as part of the common reality.

It is not the map of difference that is important, so much as the revelations of tacit assumptions and misperceptions about how things and people fit together during its construction. The architecture of the interactions enables a different sort of conversation to take place.

At a governors' meeting at an English infant school, convened to review the past year and plan the coming year, it was felt that the usual practice of splitting the governors into sub-groups to look at four areas – finance, staffing, curriculum and community communication – provided no opportunity for any of the governors to see the 'whole picture'. A complexity brainstorm was organized to address the problem.

Participants found the atmosphere created by the rules rather strange, so there was much testing of assumptions and guarding of responses, but the sub-groups duly produced their diagrams for the whole group. Those of the finance and staffing groups were virtually identical, but the maps of the curriculum and community groups were totally different, both from each other and from the finance and staffing diagrams.

The differences were thrown into sharp relief when two mixed groups were asked to plan an event in the year 2000 designed to celebrate the school's achievements. They had to consider who should be involved and how the occasion should look and feel. Some passing references were made to staffing problems, but neither group mentioned finance once, and the celebrations were remarkably similar, consisting largely of the wonderful things the children were learning and the very healthy state of community relations.

It seemed that although community and curriculum were pretty remote from the current reality, they were widely seen as the school's life-blood. Curriculum and community could no longer be regarded as incidental to planning – they had to be at the centre of the process, because if they were not, the governors could not help bring about the future they all wanted for the children.

Dialogue Cards

This card game, developed by Chris Blantern for the Learning Company Project, is useful in one-to-one meetings or in small groups when difference is preventing people from doing things together.

Participants are asked to express their view of a (preferably non-trivial) shared task and keep it in mind. They then take turns (symbolized by drawing cards) to talk about what to do next, but the talk is not free: it must obey the card.

The cards says things like:

- 'I want to hear your half-baked ideas – and I'll tell you mine.'
- 'I don't know what's best for you.'
- 'I listen to what I'm saying.'
- 'My questions flow from my curiosity rather than my desire to steer you.'
- 'In what ways do I fault you, in order to minimize the validity of your story or view?'
- 'If I'm uncertain, I don't try to cover it up.'

Participants can either a draw a card for their own talk or can agree to play a card on behalf of someone else. Readers might like to ask themselves whether any of the above legends might have been helpful in a recent situation they were involved in where difference seemed to be an issue.

The Dialogue Circle

Developed by the Re-View partnership, the Dialogue Circle was designed for groups of up to 25 people.

Participants are first invited to describe the 'futures' they see, focusing on the sort of future they, as individuals, can subscribe to. A second conversation takes place to enable all the stories of the future to be heard and the collaborative space to be mapped. This second regulated dialogue provides a structure for the group to move from a picture of the future to a series of communally agreeable actions in the present.

Participants are asked to write their suggestions for actions on cards (one suggestion per card, three cards per person). A circle is formed, and participants take turns to read out the suggestions on their cards and then place them in the centre. Others can 'remove' the card if they feel unable or unwilling to take or support the step it suggests. The rule is that if it stays in the centre, it will happen.

The only speaking allowed at this stage in the process is the reading out of the cards. Once the reading out and removal of cards is complete, people can say what they want, on condition that they first state the purpose of what they want to say. This is not easy to comply with, and is not intended for everyday conversations. It is an intervention mechanism that determines who gets to speak, who gets to be heard, who gets to control the topic, and who gets control of whom in pursuit of which outcomes.

So, for example, the conversation may begin with a participant wishing to challenge the removal of a particular card. There are many possible motivations for such a challenge, ranging from a suspicion that the card has been removed in order to block a particular line of conversation or action to a wish to know whether the card could be made acceptable by a change of wording.

The requirement to make purpose explicit obliges speakers to think carefully about what they are trying to achieve (in terms of the actions proposed, and the conversation) before saying anything.

Someone might say, for example, 'The purpose of this is to find out why you removed my card. Was it because you don't want to see my suggestion happen?', to which the answer might be: 'The purpose of this is to assure you that I support the idea, but would like us to look at the words. I took it out because the way it is worded makes me think we're taking too much on.' Alternatively, someone might say, 'The purpose of this is to check whether you support the basic idea, as I imagine you do. Why did you take the card out?', to which an answer might be: 'The purpose of this is to tell you that you've got that wrong. I took the card out because I don't think the idea will work.'

The system gives people a structured way of checking out each other's assumptions and purposes, and so enables decisions to be reached that everyone supports. No one is forced to say anything they are not willing to say, but the space is there for being honest about purpose: one of the basic preconditions of trust. This finesses the normal conversational conventions about saving the face of those who have the most power, maintaining the appearance of agreement or consensus which usually leads to a great deal of lip service but very little action.

Members are asked to look again at the cards they removed, to establish whether they are 'common ground', possible projects or just 'not agreed'. Common ground suggestions are acted on straight away, and this action often leads to a reassessment of removed cards.

The Dialogue Circle structure can be used by agreement – when everyone present takes responsibility for keeping the rules – whenever a group needs to establish priorities or decide what to do next about any matter, ranging from the future of their organizations to the agenda of a difficult meeting.

References

Jacobs, R.W. (1994) *Real-time Strategic Change*, Berrett-Koehler.

Owen, H. (1992) *Riding the Tiger: Doing Business in a Transforming World*, Abbott Publishing.

Revans, R. (1980) *Action Learning: New Techniques for Management*, Blond & Briggs.

Weisbord, M. et al. (1992) *Discovering Common Ground*, Berrett-Koehler.

Index